Inclusion

Inclusion: Developing an Effective Whole School Approach

Alison Ekins and Peter Grimes

Open University Press

Open University Press
McGraw-Hill Education
McGraw-Hill House
Shoppenhangers Road
Maidenhead
Berkshire
England
SL6 2QL

email: enquiries@openup.co.uk
world wide web: www.openup.co.uk

and Two Penn Plaza, New York, NY 10121–2289, USA

First published 2009

A catalogue record of this book is available from the British Library

ISBN-13: 978-0-33-5236046 (pb) 978-0-33-5236053 (hb)
ISBN-10: 0-33-523604-9 (pb) 0-33-523605-7 (hb)

Typeset by Kerrypress, Luton, Bedfordshire
Printed and bound in the UK by Bell and Bain Ltd, Glasgow

Mixed Sources
Product group from well-managed
forests and other controlled sources
www.fsc.org Cert no. TT-COC-002769
© 1996 Forest Stewardship Council
FSC

The McGraw·Hill Companies

We have worked with many schools that are striving to develop more inclusive practices to support the participation, enjoyment and achievement of all pupils. This book is dedicated to them.

Contents

Preface

This book is based on our extensive work with schools in recent years, all of whom have been trying to develop more inclusive practices in order to meet the needs of all their pupils.

A number of systems and processes have emerged and are currently being advocated through the National Strategies, the Department for Children, Schools and Families (DCSF) and Ofsted, which we believe are powerful tools to encourage inclusive practices within schools. We have seen, however, how schools have struggled to engage fully with the number of new initiatives in an inclusive and meaningful way. Practitioners and school leaders have at times lost sight of the central and guiding principles behind the various approaches and systems – and in doing so, these become meaningless paper-based activities rather than the strategic tools for whole school development that they can become.

We are both committed to developing inclusive principles and practices within schools and supporting schools to engage fully in a range of systems and processes which can enhance strategic planning to meet the needs of all pupils.

Although there is some guidance about the whole school systems and processes within Ofsted, DCSF and National Strategy, practitioners have found that there is a need for further materials which provide a more objective and critical perspective, and which can contextualize the processes within an overall philosophy of inclusive education. This is what we aim to provide within this book.

This book is not intended as a prescriptive 'how-to' manual or guide. However, in writing it, we have tried to make it as practical and immediately accessible to practitioners as possible. We believe that for meaningful school change to happen, practitioners need to be supported to be reflective and questioning of their own practice and of new initiatives and agendas. Only when there is a critical mass of staff within school settings who are willing to engage in professional discourse can new and innovative ways forward be discovered.

We have therefore utilized a number of strategies and approaches to our writing and presentation of the ideas to enable readers to start this process of reflection. In particular we have used case studies and reflective or contextual questions.

The case studies and questions are purposefully generic. We have used our experiences with a range of both secondary and primary schools to develop case studies, and reflective questions which could be used and adapted to suit the learning and development needs of both secondary and primary staff. Many of the issues are similar for both primary and secondary contexts, and we would encourage staff to use the information and examples to reflect upon their own particular contexts.

The approach we are advocating is a model of whole school development which attempts to unify different processes and systems and which we call *Inclusion in*

Action. The way in which Inclusion in Action works is dynamic in that it enables the interlinking of processes which are often seen as separate. In each school the exact model will look slightly different, and will reflect different patterns of working. However, for many schools operating at Stage 3 of our model, the different processes will occur simultaneously, working to complement and enhance each other. We would like to acknowledge to the readers that, because of this, it has been difficult to decide how to structure the book. By arranging the chapters in a particular order, we are aware that we perhaps seem to emphasize certain aspects of the model over others, or are suggesting a linear order to be followed. However, this is not the case. As is made clear in Chapters 1 and 2, schools must find their own starting points for school development.

We hope that schools will use this book and adapt the ideas and strategies in a way that best suits their context. It is designed to support the inclusion of all pupils in school and we hope that after reading the book practitioners will introduce activities and engage in processes in different ways and will ask themselves three key questions:

- Are our pupils enjoying school more than they were?
- Are they participating more than they were?
- Are they learning and achieving more than they were?

If the answer to any or all of these questions is 'yes' then the book will have done its job!

Alison Ekins and Peter Grimes
Canterbury
February 2009

Acknowledgements

Our thanks go to our families who have supported us through the process of writing this book – Andy, Joseph, Jacob, Charlotte, Samuel, Ann and Chris; Barbara, Mei and Ani – and to Mei for her expertise in MS Word without which the Inclusion in Action model may never have made it onto paper!

We would also like to acknowledge our gratitude to our colleagues on the Kent County Council Inclusion and Achievement Advisory Team. In particular, Alwen Coventry, whose work has been fundamental in developing this book.

We would like to thank the hundreds of schools and staff members that we have worked with over the last five years – without whom the ideas within the book would not have evolved so naturally. In particular, we would like to acknowledge the staff of Kingsmead Primary School in Canterbury, especially Michelle Anderson and Kate Hester; and the staff of Harbinger Primary School in Tower Hamlets, especially Mandy Boutwood and Nicky Stephenson, for their continual support and encouragement.

Finally, we would like to thank a number of colleagues whose support and writing has been fundamental to the development of ideas in the book – Mel Ainscow, Maggie Balshaw, Andy Howes, Jenny Corbett, Judy Durrant and Avril Crane.

1 Inclusion in Action

In this chapter we critically explore the following issues and concepts:

- Introducing a model of Inclusion in Action
- Key educational issues impacting upon the evolution of the model of Inclusion in Action
- School development, self-evaluation and inclusion
- Key principles in developing inclusive approaches within schools
- The three stages of inclusive school development
- Stages of development leading to the model of Inclusion in Action

Introducing a model of Inclusion in Action

In this book we aim to tackle the fundamental issue of how schools inclusively meet the needs of all their pupils. We argue that there needs to be a more coherent approach to whole school evaluation and development and present a model of Inclusion in Action which draws together different systems and processes into a coherent whole school approach. Schools must ask themselves how they are ensuring they are meeting the needs of all their pupils.

The model that we develop and describe within this book draws from our extensive experiences supporting a range of schools to work more effectively and inclusively with school-based systems and processes. Our aim throughout all of our work is to support schools to become more inclusive places by helping practitioners to understand the values and principles behind what can often be considered to be paper-based activities. These include systems such as provision mapping, data analysis and pupil tracking and target setting.

Inclusion in Action encourages the development of joined-up thinking in schools, which sees all children as complex individuals with the right to participate and achieve fully. We argue that this should occur within school systems which exist to serve and reflect upon children's holistic development (Corbett 2001). Schools are most effective when everybody from the head teacher and senior leadership team through to teachers, teaching assistants and governors is fully involved and understands self-evaluation and school development processes.

In order to help practitioners to engage effectively in responding to and meeting the needs of groups of learners vulnerable to experiencing barriers, we emphasize the need for schools to develop meaningful strategic approaches to the development of a range of whole school systems such as self-evaluation, data tracking and analysis, provision mapping, intervention planning and target setting. These systems are not new. Most of them have been identified by the Office for Standards in Education (Ofsted; 2004a), the Department for Children, Schools and Families (DCSF) and the National Strategies – both at primary and secondary level – as examples of good practice. However, although many schools are engaging with the systems in different ways, this is frequently because they are required to do so rather than because they fully understand their potential. The systems are often seen as simple, paper-based activities or as a means to an end. The value that the systems hold for enabling innovative, meaningful and strategic whole school development can be lost.

We want to support practitioners to be able to see the different systems in a more dynamic and practical way. Our work enables practitioners to visualize ways to make important links between these systems, rather than seeing them as separate processes which are completed by different staff members within the school setting. We argue that schools can make the processes much more meaningful and valuable by engaging with them in a more holistic way.

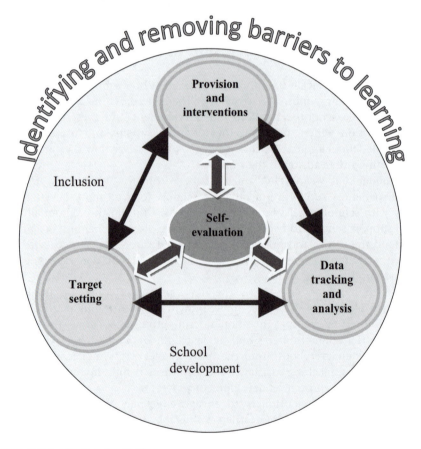

Figure 1.1 Inclusion in Action

The model is a series of interlinking processes set within an overall inclusive focus of identifying and removing barriers to learning (see Figure 1.1). These interlinking processes draw together the three broad educational fields of inclusion, school development and self-evaluation. Schools need to understand the importance of linking all three fields in a dynamic way to drive the development of more inclusive practices. Inclusion cannot move forward effectively within schools without rigorous and meaningful self-evaluation at all levels of the school community (MacBeath 2006). Self-evaluation is therefore at the centre of Inclusion in Action. Linked to this are the systems and processes which we suggest should be carried out at a whole school level, to respond to and meet the needs of all pupils. These include pupil tracking and data analysis of pupil progress, intervention and provision planning and target setting. By linking these systems and processes together within a dynamic model of whole school development, the school is supported to identify trends and patterns of progress or underachievement and can then more effectively identify and set appropriate priorities for whole school development.

It should be noted here that Inclusion in Action responds to the unique nature of the individual school context, and thus a prescriptive list of particular activities to complete is not provided. Rather, we suggest ways to start to think about how to link relevant and essential school systems into a whole school development model which can then respond to the particular needs and issues arising directly out of the school context.

Key educational issues impacting upon the evolution of the model of Inclusion in Action

A number of key issues within the current educational system have influenced our thinking, leading to the evolution of our model of Inclusion in Action. We present and briefly discuss them here.

Balancing an inclusive approach to education with the reality of government agendas

Our work is embedded in an inclusive approach to education. We also acknowledge the practical realities for schools that are trying to develop more inclusive practices under great pressure from a standards agenda imposed by central government. We believe it is the duty of all teachers and schools to work together actively to identify and remove potential barriers to the participation, engagement and achievement of all pupils in their local community schools. However, this view of inclusion is contested and sometimes at odds with other interpretations based on models of special needs and disability. In England, the government Department for Children, Schools and Families (DCSF) and national inspection body Ofsted have compounded this confusion, issuing guidance and reports to schools clearly linking inclusion with special needs agendas (Ofsted 2006a).

Inclusion and achievement

Linked closely to the above is the problematic tension between competing national policy expectations for developing more inclusive practices while at the same time promoting the raising of standards. Coming to a common agreement and understanding about the meaning of achievement is problematic and yet notions of achievement and measuring progress underpin many of the systems we explore in this book. In our work with schools we find that many teachers are struggling to make sense of their own view of achievement based on pupils developing broadly as individuals and achieving as highly as they are able to, within a policy context in which achievement is increasingly measured by simplistic outcome-based measurements in the most valued areas of the curriculum, namely literacy and numeracy. For schools trying to develop an increasingly inclusive environment, a clear tension exists within national policy which promotes the inclusion of children identified as having special educational needs in mainstream settings while at the same time focusing upon raising attainment. The tension between these two positions has been articulated by the House of Commons Select Committee for Education and Skills in their report on special educational needs (House of Commons 2006) where they make the point that 'the evidence clearly demonstrates that SEN and the raising attainment agenda sit very uncomfortably together at present' (2006: 66).

Current national systems for measuring pupil achievement are limited in their scope. They do not acknowledge the quality of work that most schools do in supporting the all-round development of pupils. We also believe that the impact of national testing has been to narrow the curriculum in many schools and to encourage exclusionary pedagogies such as fixed ability groupings in classrooms, setting and segregationary practices when implementing interventions to support those who are not achieving to national expected norms. Yet schools are compelled to find a way through these tensions and provide evidence that they are improving and meeting national targets. We believe that developing more inclusive practice does mean raising achievement across the school and that this can be very powerful and creative (Hart *et al.* 2004). We also acknowledge that this is challenging for many schools. We hope that the material in this book supports them in trying to develop creative ways to support pupils to achieve highly across the curriculum as well as in core subjects.

Refreshing the principles within the English National Curriculum inclusion statement

Within the English National Curriculum, there is a clear statement of inclusion, which describes the statutory duty for all teachers teaching in mainstream schools to be proactive in ensuring that they meet the learning needs of all pupils. We believe that this inclusion statement embodies some of the underlying core values and principles behind any attempt to drive forward inclusion and the development of meaningful inclusive practice. The inclusion statement in the English National Curriculum for Key Stages 1 and 2 (primary age children between the ages of 5 and 11 years of age), sets out three principles that are essential for teachers and schools to follow when developing an inclusive curriculum:

- setting suitable learning challenges;
- responding to pupils' diverse learning needs;
- overcoming potential barriers to learning and assessment for individuals and groups of pupils.

(DES 1999)

Whilst the importance of these three principles is key within our conceptualization of inclusion, in reality many schools and teachers are not clear about these principles or sufficiently familiar with them. Often these vital key principles are lost or buried under competing initiatives or agendas, and therefore do not form the basis for all thinking about teaching within the English educational system. We would argue that these principles remain valid, but that there is now a need to refresh them within the minds and thinking of all practitioners.

There is a wide range of research which indicates that one of the most effective ways to develop inclusive practice is through a whole school emphasis on inclusive culture, policy and practice in schools (Corbett 2001; Booth and Ainscow 2002; Kugelmass 2004; Ainscow *et al.* 2006). By reinvigorating these three principles and by considering them within the context of the interactive and dynamic model which we present later, we hope that practitioners and whole school communities may find further ways to engage with the complex issue of developing meaningful inclusive practice to support the needs of all pupils.

Every Child Matters – Change for Children

The 2004 Children Act (DfES 2004b) was designed to radically change educational and social provision for all children. It has led to the reorganization of all local authority services for children into Children's Trusts; created a policy framework based around five key outcomes; and changed the inspection framework for joint services so that it measures institutional performance in meeting these. It is difficult to argue with the central notion that *every child matters*, because of course this is true. On the surface there may also be little to dispute in the actual titles of the five outcomes:

- Staying healthy
- Keeping safe
- Enjoying and achieving
- Contributing to community
- Social and economic well-being

However, as with the notion of inclusion and achievement, there is much here that is problematic and which creates tensions and challenges for schools in translating policy and rhetoric into practice. MacBeath has argued, at the onset of the Every

Child Matters (ECM) change, that the new approach would 'acknowledge that achievement is a more far-reaching notion than test scores and that schools are not solely responsible for pupil outcomes' (MacBeath 2006). ECM led directly to a new Ofsted inspection framework and a much heralded new relationship with schools, based on self-evaluation around the five outcomes. Five years on, there should have been enough time for these changes to bed in and for there to have been a marked improvement in service delivery for children and significant changes in the way in which schools work with their pupils. However, despite MacBeath's optimism, schools are still judged very much on the extent to which pupils achieve national benchmarks and there is still evidence that joined-up service delivery across England faces significant challenges in achieving the expectations laid out in the Children Act.

We do not intend to provide a commentary on ECM throughout this book, or to make links continuously between the approaches we suggest and the Children Act agenda. We hope that the reader understands that the five outcomes underpin much of our work and while we acknowledge the tensions and challenges schools face in actually delivering these changes, we generally support the principles behind them.

School development, self-evaluation and inclusion

Inclusion in Action draws upon three broad fields that are prevalent within educational discourse. These are:

- school development;
- self-evaluation;
- inclusion.

These three phrases convey a range of different meanings to readers. On the face of it, it is possible to look at the three terms, all of which are familiar and well used within current education rhetoric both in the UK and internationally, and argue that they are all clearly understood within most schools. However, our experience is that there is much confusion surrounding the three and, furthermore, very little understanding in schools of how the three link together and support each other. It is therefore essential that, before progressing further, we clearly articulate and present our thinking in relation to each of these terms. This will then inform the principles which underpin each chapter.

It is not our intention to provide a comprehensive overview of these ideas. This would be a far longer book than we are trying to write and there are also several books which provide a more detailed overview (Stoll and Fink 1996; Ainscow *et al.* 2006; MacBeath 2006). However, in this introductory section of the book, we will place our ideas in a context which draws together these different threads. Our aim is to demonstrate how the dynamic model we present draws together these three agendas and initiatives.

School development

We choose the phrase 'school development' rather than 'school effectiveness' or 'school improvement' because it reinforces the idea that schools are complex social contexts where any initiatives to change practice must be seen as a developmental process. Whilst we support the concept of schools wanting to improve or become more effective, there are concerns that often 'school improvement' or 'effectiveness' can be perceived as uncontested terms. We see school development as a problematic process that needs to be clearly linked to school review at all levels of the school. It can be argued that there are clear differences in meaning between these different terms, for example that school effectiveness is concerned with 'what' we try to change and school improvement focuses on 'how' we try to change it (Stoll and Fink 1996), while school development might be seen as a more generic term to describe the overall process. We also choose school development because school improvement and effectiveness seem to have become closely linked to the standards agenda.

Self-evaluation

We examine school self-evaluation in more detail in Chapter 2 but it is important to be clear that, for us, self-evaluation is not just about meeting Ofsted inspection framework requirements (Ofsted 2005). Because self-evaluation is a requirement for all English schools, there is an assumption that teachers and school leaders have at least a reasonable understanding of what the process entails. Our work with schools indicates that this is not the case. In many schools we have found that self-evaluation is often geared to completion of the online School Evaluation Form or SEF, a process usually under the ownership of the head teacher and sometimes, but not always, the senior leadership team. Consultation with the school community may involve a brief yearly questionnaire for parents and children and 'sharing' the SEF with teachers in a staff meeting.

We do not believe this is a very effective form of self-evaluation. We advocate an ongoing, reflective process engaging all members of the school community in taking ownership of the evaluation of the school's development. We also believe that this self-review should be clearly linked to the core values and ethos of the school community, examining key questions such as 'What are we aiming to achieve in our school?' and 'What kind of school community do we aspire to be?' These questions should be based on the core inclusive value of equality: the rights of all children (UN 1989) to a quality education that meets their needs – social, emotional and academic.

This connection between self-evaluation and inclusion is based, in part, upon the approach to school development described in the *Index for Inclusion* (Booth and Ainscow 2002). It should be clear that our work is embedded in an inclusive approach to education based on the work of writers such as Mel Ainscow, Tony Booth and Jenny Corbett (Ainscow 1999; Corbett 2001; Booth and Ainscow 2002; Ainscow *et al.* 2006).

SEN to inclusion: moving towards whole school approaches

There has been a marked increase in the use of the phrases 'inclusion', 'inclusive education' and 'inclusive schools' in international literature, policy and rhetoric (Corbett 2001; Peters 2003; Singal 2005). This would seem in part to be due to the impact of the Salamanca statement (UNESCO 1994) and the argument that:

> ... regular schools with an inclusive orientation are ... the most effective means of combating discriminatory attitudes, building an inclusive society and achieving education for all.

> (UNESCO 1994)

However, 'inclusion' has also become a subject of debate internationally (Dyson *et al.* 2002) and the concept has acquired what has been referred to as 'jet lag' (Slee 2004). That is to say, the phrase has become tired and confused and lost its clarity, meaning different things to different people.

Based on our work with schools, we would identify three different views of inclusion which are commonly used:

1. A focus on disability and special educational needs.
2. A focus on challenging behaviour.
3. A focus on vulnerable groups.

Ainscow *et al.* (2006) expand upon this list and have developed a more extended Typology of Inclusion, which we would recommend to readers wishing to explore these ideas further.

A focus on disability and special educational needs

Inclusion for many professionals is inextricably linked with special educational needs. Recent reports on inclusion commissioned by the National Union of Teachers in England (MacBeath *et al.* 2005), the NASUWT Teaching Union in England (Ellis *et al.* 2008), Ofsted (2004a, 2006a), and guidance produced by National Strategy (DfES 2005) all associate the term with special educational needs and disability. The term 'special educational needs' reinforces a medical model of disability, where impairments, difficulties, barriers to learning and participation are located within the child. However, this view of inclusion does not equate with a social model of disability which argues that the problems that children with disabilities experience in school are the result of inflexible policies and practices. It is possible to view inclusion as being concerned with the rights of disabled pupils to attend mainstream settings (Peters 2003), but one of the main problems with this is that, for some, linking inclusion and special needs will always tend to reinforce the view that there will be some pupils who need specialist, segregated provision. Linking inclusion with special educational needs prevents many schools thinking beyond 'labels' of difficulty (Hart 1996) and addressing the barriers that they themselves may be creating to pupils' learning through their practice.

A focus on challenging behaviour

For many teachers, the term 'inclusion' will often be associated with 'exclusion'. Our work with schools, will often begin with anxious teachers complaining about pupils with challenging behaviour whom the teachers feel 'shouldn't be here' even though they are expected to be 'included'. This finding was echoed by the NUT report (MacBeath *et al.* 2005). Where these pupils should be instead is never quite made clear to us, and perhaps is a symptom of some teachers being unable to see beyond their own setting. Nevertheless, this is a frequent reaction in schools to any discussion about developing more inclusive practices.

We feel that disciplinary exclusions reinforce a medical model of behaviour difficulties in that they focus attention on the 'behavioural' difficulties of the child rather than examining the school systems, culture and practices which may be inherently 'exclusionary'. However, we also acknowledge that there are some children who need a far more comprehensive response on a community/social level as well as in school to enable them to participate fully and achieve in school. This should not be an excuse for schools to 'pass the problem' on to other professionals. Rather it should be seen as an opportunity for services to provide a truly joined-up approach (DfES 2004b, 2004c) which puts pupils and their families firmly in the centre of the process.

A focus on vulnerable groups

The notion of inclusion as being concerned with vulnerable groups has become more common internationally (Grimes 2009) as well as in the UK. Ofsted have identified a number of specific groups of children who they argue are most likely to experience underachievement, or barriers to learning and participation. Although there are certain disadvantages to the vulnerable groups approach to inclusion, we believe it can support a rights-based examination of school culture, policy and practice and is often a useful way of enabling teachers in schools to engage practically with developing more inclusive practice. However, there can be a tendency to develop isolated strategies in relation to different vulnerable groups, which can often lead to segregationary practices (Doreman *et al.* 2005). This is discussed in more detail in Chapter 3.

Whilst we have noted evidence of all these different views of inclusion being applied in schools in the UK and internationally, we believe that it is more useful for schools to aim to develop a shared understanding of inclusion as a principled approach to education and society (Ainscow *et al.* 2006). For many, inclusion is increasingly being interpreted as a broad, rights-based concept concerned with identifying and removing barriers to participation and achievement for all pupils

(Booth and Ainscow 2002). It requires that all schools seek to maximize the participation of all in school systems and often demands radical changes within schools (Barton 1997).

Key principles in developing inclusive approaches within schools

The development of an inclusive school is underpinned by a focus on the development of inclusive cultures which permeate the life of the school (Corbett 2001), around inclusive values which inform the development of a curriculum and pedagogy which responds to the diversity of all learners (Hart *et al.* 2004), and the involvement and engagement of all stakeholders, staff, pupils, parents and local community (Carrington and Robinson 2006: 332).

Developing inclusive school cultures

Our experience of working with schools indicates that there is often a serious gap between the inclusive policies in the school, which may contain the ideas outlined above, and the actual practices observed in classrooms and around the school. Because of this we believe that schools wishing to develop inclusive practice need to focus not only on developing inclusive policies but also on developing inclusive cultures (Booth and Ainscow 2002). The development of policies, practice and school culture are inextricably linked and depend upon the engagement of the whole school community.

Responding to pupil diversity

The *Index for Inclusion* (Booth and Ainscow 2002) encourages schools to consider the curriculum, culture, policy and practice of their school community and to focus on school development initiatives which embrace pupil diversity. The implication of this view is that inclusive schools are ones which focus on good quality teaching and learning experiences for all pupils (Corbett 2001; Kugelmass 2004) but do *not* focus on the achievement of particular groups in any way that risks increasing their social exclusion by offering segregated differentiated support (Doreman *et al.* 2005).

Developing leaders who are committed to inclusive values

Inclusive schools will tend to have leaders committed to inclusive values and there are also likely to be a range of individuals within the school community who participate in leadership roles or functions (Dyson *et al.* 2002). This is a form of distributive leadership (NCSL 2004) aiming to facilitate the learning of all pupils. This leadership is not just confined to adults but should also involve pupils taking on some aspects of the leadership role as well (Lambert *et al.*, cited in Kugelmass 2004). Research points to the importance of school head teachers or principals who are committed to a vision for the school that incorporates inclusive ideals and values (Ainscow 1999; Corbett 2001; Kugelmass, 2004). The significance of such commitment highlights the limitations of rhetoric or following an agenda set by others at local or national level (Carrington and Robinson 2006).

'Evolving shared inclusive values

Sustainability and shared leadership depends partly on the nature of the staff group within the school, their relationships with one another, their commitment to the inclusive values of the school and the school's shared vision (Ainscow 1999; Corbett 2001; Booth and Ainscow 2002; Kugelmass 2004; Carrington and Robinson 2006). It also seems clear that there needs to be a 'critical mass' (Kugelmass 2004: 67) of teachers who are committed to these values, to maintaining good working relationships with each other and the school community as a whole.

Developing collaborative problem solving

The ethos of the school needs also to reflect a commitment to collaborative problem solving (Hanko 1999). A legacy of the application of the medical model of disability in educational settings has been the misconception that students with *special* educational needs need *specialist* support and intervention. A recent review of research on teachers' perceptions of SEN found that specialist knowledge and skills were seen as very important and there was a general perception in English schools that more training for all teachers was necessary (Ellis *et al.* 2008). Whilst there is undoubtedly a need for teachers to develop key skills and a wider understanding of the specific challenges that some pupils face in schools, the notion of a specialized pedagogy for SEN deflects our attention away from the need to focus on ways in which the school teaching and learning context can be explored to find solutions to challenges. Hanko's work in this area (Hanko 1995, 1999) has emphasized the value of collaborative problem-solving approaches which bring together parents and professionals in a non-hierarchical reflective structure where different perspectives are explored with an aim of finding ways forward without imposing so-called *professionalized expertise* onto discussions.

Individual inclusive school development

It is important to note that research also indicates that there is not a 'blueprint' model for developing inclusive schools. It does not appear that it is possible to apply the processes undertaken by successful inclusive schools to those seeking to develop inclusive practice (Pirrie and Brna 2006; Booth and Black-Hawkins 2001, 2005) and expect replication. This is because of the complexity of school communities and the reality that, because of circumstances, contexts and agendas at personal, school, local and national level, it is impossible for two schools to be exactly the same. This seems to be borne out by research which suggests that there tends to be 'pockets of innovation' (Carrington and Robinson 2006: 332), with exceptional schools making great progress while others locally are struggling (Corbett 2001).

We also feel it is important to acknowledge that any typology of inclusion cannot be applied as a simple measurement of 'inclusion' but should, rather, be seen as a model for exploring what inclusive development means in the context of individual schools (Singal and Rouse 2003: 87).

In summary, the key principles that inform the development of Inclusion in Action within individual school contexts are listed in the box below.

Inclusion in Action – what can it look like within a school?

- An inclusive culture which builds upon shared understanding of and commitment to inclusive values and practices.
- An ethos which is built upon removing barriers to participation, access and achievement for all pupils.
- School leaders who have a strong commitment to inclusive values – and there is evidence of distributed leadership across the school.
- All children enjoy school and the importance of this is valued by everyone.
- The curriculum has been designed to meet the needs of all.
- Diversity is recognized and celebrated.
- All staff are fully involved and work collaboratively together on whole school systems and processes which are linked in dynamic ways.
- There is ongoing professional and reflective dialogue which focuses on problem solving and developing creative approaches to curriculum innovation.
- Partnership working with parents and the local community is a priority.
- There is a creative and professional approach to working collaboratively with a wide range of other professionals and agencies to support the needs of all pupils.

Building upon these guiding principles, we now present the Inclusion in Action model which supports practitioners in developing their thinking about ways to engage with the issues in an increasingly meaningful and effective way. We believe that there are three discrete stages of development in relation to this. The Inclusion in Action model that we have developed sits within the last of these three stages of development.

The three stages of inclusive school development

During the last ten years thinking and practice in England has led to more of an emphasis upon demonstrating that all children are making progress in school. Schools have had to develop a range of systems and processes to enable them to effectively track, monitor, analyse and review the progress of all pupils and to measure the impact and quality of the provision and interventions that are on offer within the school setting.

These processes include the following:

- **Data collection** – The introduction of national testing in England in 1988 has led to an increasing focus on school performance, measurable through pupil performance in SATs. Most schools now have effective systems to collect levels and scores which measure pupil progress at regular points through the year.
- **Data analysis** – Once data has been collected relating to levels of pupil progress, most schools have developed systems which enable them to look at and analyse key trends in terms of pupil outcomes across the school and in different areas of the curriculum.
- **Pupil tracking** – Using the systems developed within the data collection and data analysis stages, staff members can track the progress of individual pupils to ensure that appropriate and effective levels of progress are sustained.
- **Target setting** – In England, all pupils are required to have class-based targets set for English, maths and science, and schools have developed a range of ways to ensure that the targets that are set are meaningful, are reviewed on a regular basis, and help to ensure effective pupil outcomes. Children who are placed on the SEN register also require high-quality targets to be set and reviewed on a regular basis in order to meet their individual and different needs.
- **Intervention planning/provision mapping** – Schools plan a range of quality interventions and provisions to support pupils in achieving their targets, and to help them make good rates of progress. Many schools across England use provision mapping systems to enable them to plan strategically in order to respond to needs across the school.
- **Self-evaluation** – Schools now play a more active role in the evaluation and inspection process and, as part of the New Relationship with Schools (Ofsted 2004b) are required to complete an online self-evaluation form (SEF) which is used to inform Ofsted inspections. Self-evaluation within our model incorporates the whole school SEF, but extends this to include other whole school evaluation activities and opportunities which help to impact upon each of the other systems described above, and which also act as the vehicle to drive forward the other two broad educational fields, school development and inclusion.

Taking some time to consider the reflective questions below will help practitioners to think about current practices within their school and to identify future priorities for action.

Reflective questions	Comments – identifying priorities for action for my practice and my school
How is the process of self-evaluation undertaken within your school? Who is involved? When does this occur? What activities have been developed to encourage and engage participation from all members of the school community? Are there any stakeholders who are currently not fully involved e.g. school staff/pupils/parents/the wider school community?	
Does your school engage in processes such as target setting, intervention planning, pupil tracking and data analysis? How is this organized? Who is involved? How do the individual processes relate to each other? How do the processes impact upon pupil learning and engagement within the school? How do the processes lead to future strategic planning and development for the whole school to respond to developing needs?	
What do you perceive your role to be in enabling the processes to occur within your school setting? Will you lead developments as a Senior Leader? How will you collaborate/work in strategic partnership with colleagues? Will you support other schools to think in different ways about the issues raised? Will you contribute to whole school self-evaluation?	

Stages of development leading to the model of Inclusion in Action

Stage 1

In Stage 1, schools tend to see the systems as discrete and only tentatively connected with each other. Different staff members may be responsible for the different processes or systems, with little or no interaction and discussion between personnel about how each impacts upon another. Often the processes may be viewed as paper-based activities which need to be completed to satisfy external requirements. Each of the systems is timetabled to occur at particular times in the school calendar, and once completed can be 'ticked off' while staff attention moves on to the next activity to be completed.

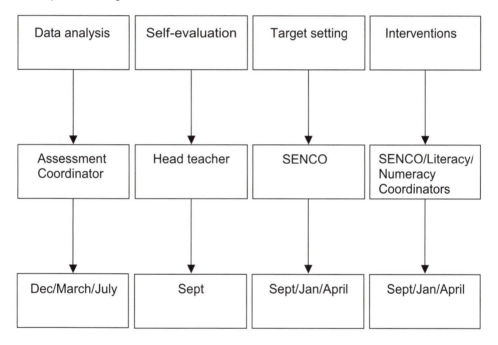

Stage 1 case study

Individual members of staff within the school have attended training courses which have highlighted the need for schools to track and analyse data in different ways.

The SENCO has received training about his or her statutory duties under the Code of Practice, and regularly reviews the SEN register, informing parents if and when their child is placed upon the SEN register. He or she also meets with teachers three times a year to discuss, review and set Individual Education Plan

(IEP) targets. The SENCO also line manages the teaching assistants and decides who will deliver different intervention programmes. The SENCO has received specialized input on particular SEN-based intervention programmes, and uses this knowledge to set up intervention groups – but has not attended training about and is not aware of current National Strategy intervention programmes.

The Assessment Coordinator sets up assessment weeks three times a year, where all the children are assessed and their scores collated. The Assessment Coordinator oversees the practical organization of this, and also keeps a record of the assessment results. The Assessment Coordinator is unsure about expected rates of pupil progress or how to input and access assessment and pupil tracking data using some of the centralized computerized systems, such as Raise-Online. Instead, the secretary inputs the data and the head teacher uses it to inform the self-evaluation form.

The head teacher is responsible for the school self-evaluation form and gathers information to update the profile on an annual basis.

The Literacy and Numeracy Coordinators have attended training from National Strategy Consultants and monitor the effective delivery of the Renewed Frameworks. They are aware of some different intervention programmes which can be used to support their particular curriculum area, but are not responsible for TA allocation and do not have the time or resources to be able to oversee the setting up of these groups.

Class teachers within this school work hard to teach the children within their class, and fill in the assessment data record sheets on a regular basis, but are unaware of expected rates of pupil progress and do not use the information gathered to inform their planning or to target particular individuals or groups of children for further intervention or support.

An experienced teaching assistant within the school has for some years run speech and language skills groups with small groups of pupils and, although the catchment area of the school has changed in recent years and more children are coming to the school without the speech and language needs that used to be presented, this programme continues to be delivered without being adapted.

Stage 2

In Stage 2, schools are starting to see school development as a cyclical process using the school improvement cycle (see below) to connect some of the systems (Gross and White 2003). The cycle encourages school teams to view the development of their systems in a cyclical and joined-up way, although it does not always enable full scrutiny and consideration of the needs of vulnerable groups of pupils who may sit outside the cycle. The cycle is more about moving whole school development forward in an engaging and proactive way than about identifying or analysing individual pupil need. A feature of this stage is that schools are increasingly likely to view responsibility for the process to lie with a core team, often the senior management group within the school, and the governing body.

THE SCHOOL IMPROVEMENT CYCLE

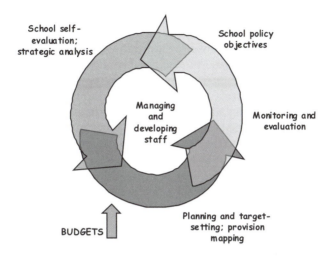

School self-evaluation; strategic analysis

School policy objectives

Managing and developing staff

Monitoring and evaluation

Planning and target-setting; provision mapping

BUDGETS

Stage 2 case study

The head teacher has developed a key group of senior teachers to form a senior management team. This team meets weekly to discuss relevant school-based issues and to agree and decide upon future actions. The information from this group, including the actions to be taken, is then passed on to the other staff during staff or teaching assistant meetings.

Members of the school management team have received training about the school improvement cycle, and are enthusiastic about using this to inform their thinking and planning.

The head teacher has implemented a cycle of monitoring and review within the school in the form of strategic lesson observations, monitoring of curriculum coverage and also work scrutiny.

Members of the senior management team have also decided to use the school improvement cycle as a way to think about development across the school, and are starting to link it to the Every Child Matters agenda. Different priorities are therefore identified each term, and the team is responsible for monitoring how the school is doing in each of the areas.

The team feed back to each other, and sometimes to the governing body, although other class teachers or members of staff have little awareness of what is being discussed within the meetings, or how key decisions regarding the school development plan are being made.

Stage 3: Inclusion in Action

In Stage 3, we present a dynamic model of whole school development. The research that has informed the development of this model is rooted in our engagement with schools across south-east England over the last eight years. In this model the systems described above are interlinked and interactive. The model is organic. In this model self-evaluation is not a once a year event, as it may be in Stage 1; self-evaluation instead becomes an ongoing process inextricably linked to the other processes of data analysis, intervention planning and so on. Rather than individual staff members (as in Stage 1) or a group of core SMT members (as in Stage 2) leading the processes, the processes become embedded within the classroom context with the class teacher taking an active and engaged part in all.

This model is founded on the development of inclusive school culture, where the active participation and achievement of every member of the school community is seen as fundamental to the ongoing successful development of the whole school.

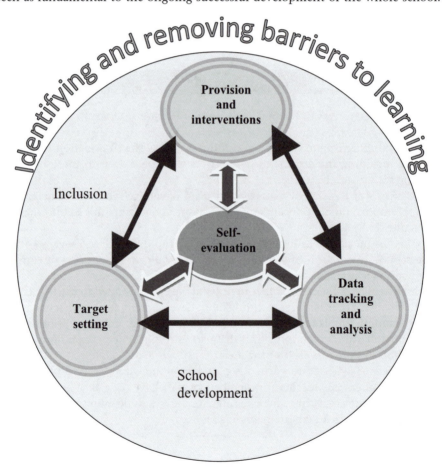

Stage 3 case study

Within this school a number of teams have been set up to work together to monitor, review and evaluate practice across the school. Opportunities are planned so that the teams can meet on a regular basis. Using the school development plan, which was put together following lengthy consultation and involvement with all stakeholders within the school (including parents, pupils, governors, teaching assistants and teaching staff) as the central plan, the head teacher is able to break the plan down into small step priorities for each team to consider, develop and feed back to the whole school community.

The teachers and teaching assistants throughout the school are enthusiastic about the priorities for action and development within the school development plan. They are knowledgeable about them and excited to be involved in their planning and development.

New and creative ideas for achieving the priorities are welcomed and considered, drawing on the strengths and different experiences of the whole school community.

Parents and pupils feel empowered and valued, and the pupils talk excitedly about decisions about the development of the school that they are involved in making.

In addition to contributing to the whole school development plan, all stakeholders are involved in an effective and meaningful process of pupil progress review.

Class teachers have a clear understanding of the assessment materials used to assess pupil progress and use these three times a year to capture levels for each child.

Once the information is collated, the head teacher plans pupil progress review meetings during which discussions about pupil outcomes and progress are discussed. Key members of the leadership team involved in planning interventions, target setting and allocating support are involved in each meeting, and the class teachers look forward to the opportunity to talk about the successes that they have had with their children as well as any gaps in progress and achievement. During the pupil progress meetings, the class teachers are encouraged to scrutinize the assessment data, and they have a clear understanding of expected levels of attainment and progress. During the meeting they are supported to identify those children who are in need of further catch-up support or intervention. A problem-solving approach is adopted during the meeting so that everyone can contribute creative and innovative ideas to move pupil progress forward. During the discussions a provision map, clearly recording planned provision and support at a whole-class, small-group and individual level is completed.

This is then used immediately to inform the class teachers' planning for the next term.

Case study 3 demonstrates that the three educational fields of inclusion, school development and self-evaluation have to interlink simultaneously in a dynamic way, in order to enable significant school change to ensure that all pupils are fully participating and achieving. This signifies a shift in thinking away from interpreting these three fields as distinct and separate.

In our model the desire to develop inclusive practice is enabled by the formulation of shared visions and values which have been negotiated through a whole school community self-evaluation process. The impact of this can lead to inclusive school development where reflection and sharing is translated into concrete action which supports all pupils in the school. This is not a linear process, as the fields interact with each other in a dynamic way. This is mirrored by the specific processes which support the development of Inclusion in Action, such as data collection, data analysis, pupil tracking, target setting, intervention planning and provision mapping, which also interact with each other dynamically.

Concluding comments

It is important for the reader to be mindful of the fact that we are not advocating a one size fits all model of whole school development. Indeed, it is essential that we acknowledge that all schools are at different stages of development, and that they will be able to respond to the ideas and examples provided here in different ways according to the ethos, culture and current working systems operating within the individual school. No two schools are the same, and it is not possible to provide a neat plan of action which will work for all schools. Instead, it will be important for readers to use the illustrative case studies and adapt them accordingly to their own school context.

The issues that we discuss and raise here are to be seen as part of an ongoing cycle and process of development. No school will ever have achieved complete perfection in terms of their inclusive practices and the systems used to support these. We would therefore encourage readers to use the case studies and supporting materials to develop reflection and critical debate and discussion within individual school contexts. By doing this, engaging the whole school community in discussion and reflection about the issues, meaningful change can occur and develop.

Throughout the book, it is this third stage of development which is discussed and emphasized.

Further examples are given to complement the brief case study outlined above and to discuss in more details issues relating to the key processes of:

- Self-evaluation (Chapter 2);
- Data Analysis (Chapter 3);
- Intervention Planning (Chapter 4);
- Provision Mapping (Chapter 5);
- Target Setting (Chapter 6).

2 Inclusive Self-Evaluation

In this chapter we critically explore the following issues and concepts:

- Self-evaluation: setting the context
- Moving from paper-based exercise to inclusive whole school development activity: principles and practice for self-evaluation
- Inclusive self-evaluation: creating a learning dialogue with staff, pupils and parents

Inclusive school self-evaluation underpins the whole school approaches we describe in this book. All of the other systems are reliant upon a whole school approach which values and prioritizes meaningful self-evaluation of existing practice and combines this with a desire to continually improve and evolve practice to meet the needs of all pupils. Our model of Inclusion in Action is concerned with the establishment of a school development and self-evaluation process in schools which places the participation of the entire school community at its centre. Schools should be aiming to ensure that all staff, students, parents and members of the wider school community are as involved as they can be in the strategic review and development of the school.

Understanding the principles behind inclusive self-evaluation will enable schools to approach Ofsted's self-evaluation framework in a new light, using the demands of the inspection requirements to develop creative and school-changing initiatives.

Self-evaluation: setting the context

What are the key principles impacting upon effective self-evaluation practices?

There has been a significant move towards greater self-evaluation of schools in England and internationally over the last two decades (Macbeath and McGlynn 2002). Self-evaluation within schools is not something new, but since Callaghan's demand in 1976 that schools be more accountable to the public (Chitty 1996) there has been an ongoing debate about the most effective ways in which to evaluate school performance. MacBeath (1999) suggested that schools should be encouraged and supported to improve and raise standards, through 'critical self-evaluation'. In order to raise levels of achievement and to develop practice, schools need to engage in in-depth, realistic and critical self-evaluation. This is school-based development which is driven internally.

Staff within the school need to be aware of the individual factors affecting progress and achievement within the school, and need to have the opportunity to understand and review the 'story' of their school: the culture and context impacting upon performance from year to year. It is

> not the mechanistic completion of progress and success checks that is important, but rather it is the enhancing of the teachers' professional judgement that is the crucial aspect of embedding an ethos of enquiry and reflection within a school

(Hopkins 2007: 110)

This depends, in part, on whole school commitment to the processes of strategic development and improvement, and this can only happen if the staff are involved in reflective and professional discussions about the nature of the learning experience within their school. This is a central issue within this book, as we seek to support practitioners to develop increasingly effective professional learning dialogues and to challenge each other critically.

Whilst this focus on recognizing an internal desire to improve (Wrigley 2003) is so important within effective self-evaluation, it is also important to note that the current context for self-evaluation does involve some form of external evaluation – usually from Ofsted. In some ways this different perspective is important, as it is argued that it enables a more objective assessment and reflection of the school's underlying strengths and weaknesses, although at times such approaches can be problematic, as is discussed within the following section.

How is the term 'self-evaluation' viewed within schools today?

In English schools, the term 'self-evaluation' has now become synonymous with new Ofsted requirements through the New Relationships with Schools framework (Ofsted 2004b) which was introduced to schools in 2004. The new Ofsted self-evaluation framework places the focus of inspection firmly upon schools' self-evaluation of their own performance. This is a move which is to be welcomed, although we would argue that the approach to self-evaluation espoused within Ofsted practice and guidance is not as inclusive as the approach that we are advocating. Meaningful self-evaluation is not just about ensuring that the school complies with Ofsted expectations regarding having a current self-evaluation form completed. We believe that it is the cornerstone for developing more inclusive practices in schools.

Schools should be encouraged to engage in approaches to self-evaluation which are contextually appropriate to their own school setting and the ways in which they currently work with systems and stakeholders. This is also a principle guiding the new Ofsted framework: 'Schools should shape for themselves a process that is simple and integrated with their routine management systems' (Ofsted 2004b).

The new self-evaluation process was not designed to be a regimented imposed national system. Rather the emphasis is upon responsiveness, again an issue which is central to the text and themes throughout this book. Even the methods of self-evaluation are not prescribed, and this is where the school should be considering practices which are best used within their context, adapting and developing them to further enhance their self-evaluation:

> The underlying process which the school employs to identify its strengths and weaknesses is not prescribed. Schools are free to follow any model which gives them the best insights into their improvement priorities.

> (Ofsted 2004b: 6)

Ofsted suggest that schools should consider how they use self-evaluation effectively:

Ofsted questions	Reflection/comment
Does the self-evaluation identify how well our school serves its learners?	
How does our school compare with the best schools, and the best comparable schools?	
Is the self-evaluation integral to our key management systems?	
Is our school's self-evaluation based on a good range of telling evidence?	
Does our self-evaluation and planning involve key people in the school and seek the views of parents, learners and external advisers and agencies?	
Does our self-evaluation lead to action to achieve the school's longer term goals for development?	

Source: Ofsted (2004: 7–10)

How does the self-evaluation form (SEF) fit in with inclusive self-evaluation?

The introduction of Ofsted's school self-evaluation form: the SEF, which replaced previous Ofsted forms S1–S4, was aimed at linking more appropriately and effectively with the new self-evaluation focus within schools. The SEF is used throughout an inspection by the inspectors, but is intended to be kept up to date and amended as needed throughout the year by the school leaders.

It is important to note that: 'Completing the SEF is not, in itself, self-evaluation. The SEF is only a place to record and summarize the findings of a thorough self-evaluation process' Ofsted, 2004b: 12). The distinction between the SEF and effective self-evaluation made by Ofsted is clear. Often, however, this distinction needs to be clarified within school settings. Schools can often get caught up in the issue of having an up-to-date and accurate SEF, but may neglect the features of effective self-evaluation which are essential to promote innovative and far-reaching school improvement and development. The balance between recording and evaluating may need to be redressed and restated to ensure that more emphasis is placed upon the sustained but essential process of in-depth self-evaluation, and that it is the knowledge gathered from that process that is then used to complete the SEF. Our experience in working with schools to support them in ongoing self-evaluation is that as the time for an expected Ofsted visit draws nearer, the focus of their energy is centred on 'how' they present themselves in the SEF. This is in contrast to ensuring that the SEF reflects a meaningful process.

Self-evaluation has developed through a system of external accountability and inspection into what should be seen as a whole school development process. It is not a paper exercise, and should not be seen as such. Instead, schools and practitioners should be encouraged to create different systems which are significant to their own practice and context, and which are embedded within the whole culture of inclusive school development and improvement. In this way, schools will be encouraged to move towards 'meaningful self-evaluation' rather than be stuck with a paper-based exercise completed because of external expectations.

Reflective questions	Reflections/comments
What systems and approaches to self-evaluation are already in place within my school setting?	

Who is involved in the current self-evaluation processes? Who else may need to be involved? Are we actively looking to engage all members of the school community? Do we encourage challenge and critique?	
How does my school view and use the two distinct processes of (a) completing an up-to-date and accurate SEF; and (b) embarking on ongoing self-evaluation?	
Are these approaches and systems only used once a year – e.g. when updating and reviewing the SEF or the school improvement plan; or are they a central part of the culture of continuous monitoring, review and evaluation within my school?	
Do the school self-evaluation processes lead to action and improvement? How does this happen?	
Is my school a 'learning school'? What do I mean by this term? Is there shared understanding of this term?	
Are we developing more inclusive practices across every aspect of the school as a result?	

Moving from paper-based exercise to inclusive whole school development activity: principles and practice for self-evaluation

What key principles are central to developing effective approaches to school self-evaluation?

Where self-evaluation is at its most effective, it moves away from being a simple paper-based activity or from being driven by external forces, towards a much more culturally based built-in model of whole school development: a model which draws together other related school improvement issues and processes in a meaningful and influential way. Much of our thinking in this area has built upon the works of John MacBeath, Tony Booth and Mel Ainscow. Schools wishing to investigate further the ideas we present, should explore their work. As starting points we would recommend: *School Inspection and Self-Evaluation: Working With the New Relationship* (MacBeath 2006) and *Index for Inclusion: Developing Learning and Participation in Schools* (Booth and Ainscow 2002).

Many of the key principles for developing effective approaches to inclusive self-evaluation mirror those outlined in Chapter 1, around developing inclusive approaches within the school setting. Evidence from Ofsted research into effective self-evaluation (Ofsted, 2006b), as well as from the work of MacBeath and others, suggests that the following principles are fundamental to success.

Leadership

The success of self-evaluation within schools is dependent upon the priority given to it by the school's leadership team. In schools where leaders are developing distributed forms of leadership, involving different members of the school community in developing 'leadership roles' and encouraging them to take responsibility for different aspects of school development, there is also more likely to be effective self-evaluation taking place.

School culture and context

Self-evaluation needs to become an integral part of the school culture, understood and engaged in by all members of the school community. The day-to-day management systems of the school must be constructed around inclusive self-evaluation processes, reflecting the individual characteristics of the school. At the heart of these systems, school leaders and staff are working together with other stakeholders, including parents, pupils, governors and the wider community. Developing this process underpins the evolution of the culture and ethos of the school so that all involved are engaged in learning dialogues in an effort to raise understanding of the issues impacting upon the quality of the teaching and learning experience for all pupils within the individual school.

Individual, school-specific approaches to self-evaluation

Where self-evaluation is at its most effective, schools have developed their own creative and innovative approaches and strategies for self-evaluation, rather than following prescriptive externally imposed systems and processes. This is linked to the argument we discussed in Chapter 1, that there is no blueprint for success. All schools are different and their self-evaluation approaches should reflect this.

Involving and engaging all stakeholders in the process

Schools with the most effective self-evaluation processes understand the need to engage with and collect the views and opinions of a range of stakeholders. These include those closely linked to the school (e.g. pupils, parents, governors) and those extended services which are becoming more closely linked to the school through the Every Child Matters and Extended Schools agendas. Although the self-evaluation process is driven from the inside, it reflects the objective views and opinions of a range of services associated with and working closely with the individual school. Self-evaluation which includes and incorporates these perspectives will help the school to move forward more effectively with evaluating new and exciting, innovative approaches to working across a range of services and with a wider range of professionals from different working practices.

Opportunities for collaborative and reflective thinking and practice

Developing reflective and challenging practitioners who are open to reflecting upon their own practice with a common desire to move thinking forward within the school is central to enhancing the potential of self-evaluation practices within the school community. We believe this is fundamental to the development of more inclusive practices in schools and explore this idea in more detail later in this chapter.

Inclusive values – making self-evaluation inclusive

In addition to the principles briefly outlined above, it is also important for schools to consider the issue of how they understand and engage with inclusive values and principles and the ways in which this enables whole school approaches to inclusive self-evaluation.

The relationship between inclusion and school development should be clarified here. We believe it is not helpful to think of schools as 'inclusive'; schools should be encouraged to work towards being as inclusive as possible. This is why we use the phrase 'developing more inclusive practice'. The process is a journey, 'an ideal to which schools can aspire but which they never reach' (Booth and Ainscow 2002: 3). It is important to understand this idea as it underpins inclusive school development and inclusive self-evaluation: these are ongoing processes. There are always new challenges and new possibilities for development. For this reason we do not agree with the idea of 'kite marks' or 'standards' for inclusion. We feel that they send out the wrong message to participants in schools, namely that not only is it possible to declare a school fully inclusive (which we do not think is possible) but also that a school can focus on being inclusive for a year or two and then move onto another priority. Schools need to think of inclusive school development as a way of focusing on all areas of school development, but through an inclusive lens (Corbett 2001). In this way, the development and self-evaluation of the school throughout each school year can focus on new priorities and challenges but always with the same ultimate aim: to improve learning and participation for everyone.

Inclusive self-evaluation is concerned with school development which seeks to improve the school through an inclusive process. In practice this means that:

- the school is developed through attention to a set of inclusive values;
- these values must reflect the views and full participation of the wider school community;
- whilst these values may differ from school to school they should be concerned with fundamental concepts such as equality, full access and participation, partnership and collaboration;
- at the heart of these values should be recognition that a cornerstone of the school's ethos is ensuring achievement, enjoyment and participation for all pupils;
- translating these ideas into practice will require
    - the active identification and removal of barriers to participation for all pupils through paying close attention to the learning environment;
    - focusing on the evolution of a truly inclusive school culture with collaboration, partnership and an evolving learning dialogue between all community members at its heart;
    - the creation of opportunities for reflection to take place about the experience of learning and participation for all students;
    - the creation of opportunities for teachers to reflect upon their own strengths and the strengths of the school as a whole.

What could be the key starting points for schools wishing to engage in inclusive self-evaluation?

There are many different ways for schools to begin thinking about inclusion and school development/self-evaluation and it is up to individual schools to identify their own priorities. Schools can utilize a number of different approaches to self-evaluation in order to choose an approach to finding a starting point that is meaningful and relevant to their particular school context.

Schools should be encouraged to consider and review the usefulness of a range of different and accessible methods:

1   **Ofsted SEF** – this provides a number of clear questions which can help school leaders and stakeholders within the school community to identify key priorities for self-evaluation and whole school development.

2   **Index for Inclusion** – a resource which supports practitioners to reflect upon different aspects of the educational and learning experience of the school community. The focus is upon removing barriers to participation for all students, and the questions which support each indicator will help practitioners to review their practice in a new light.

3   **MacBeath** – books and materials produced by MacBeath and others (see references) contain a range of practical starting points for effective self evaluation, including questions to ask of practice, as well as innovative and practical activities to use in order to engage the wider community fully within the self-evaluation process.

4   **Local authority self-evaluation tools** – many local authorities have produced and published their own tools to support schools to carry out self-evaluation of aspects of their own practice. Often this is in relation to learners with learning difficulties and disabilities (the term now used by Ofsted to replace special educational needs). We would encourage practitioners to find out more about any tools that their local authority has produced, including training or guidance to support the use of it. Where there is a narrowing of focus upon specific vulnerable groups (e.g. learners with learning difficulties and disabilities) we would suggest that the tool can be taken as a starting point to look more broadly at the educational experience of all pupils.

5   **TDA: School Improvement Planning Framework (SIPF)** – this recent guidance from the Teacher Development Agency provides an innovative approach to school improvement planning which claims to 'put the child at the centre of school improvement planning' (TDA 2007). The framework provides materials to support school practitioners to engage more meaningfully with self-evaluation and school improvement processes, and does this through a three-staged model. Within Stage 1, practitioners are encouraged to 'create a planning process based on a shared vision of where you are now, what you want to accomplish and a clear idea of how the framework can help' (TDA 2007). Stage 2 and 3 focus upon identifying objectives and ensuring successful outcomes.

The School Improvement Planning Framework explicitly states and builds upon many of the central principles within our approach. It:

- ensures broad ownership of the school improvement planning process;
- shares workload – and ownership and responsibility for school improvement planning;
- engages a wide range of stakeholders in a meaningful way;

- encourages a flexible framework to enable tools to be selected by the school to suit need and context;
- aims to create shared vision and ownership of the school's priorities;
- encourages greater participation by all staff – and thereby greater motivation, morale and thus more effective implementation.

The SIPF also looks more broadly at a range of further issues impacting upon the school, and in particular considers meaningful ways for the school to engage with the ECM and extended schools agendas.

Reflective questions	Reflections/comments
Which of the above mentioned materials and resources to support self-evaluation was I already aware of? Which of them are used meaningfully within my school context?	
Are there any that I did not previously know about? Is there anyone in the school community who may have more information about it? Is there anyone in the wider educational service that may be able to help me to find out more?	

How can engaging with school-based evidence help to inform meaningful school self-evaluation?

An important part of inclusive self-evaluation is to find starting points and then to view them through an inclusive lens – namely by asking questions of it which relate to inclusive values. Fundamental to this would be asking how the particular system or aspect of school life supports, or creates barriers to, participation for all. In doing so schools will need to engage with different forms of evidence.

Gross and White (2003) introduce the practitioner to the idea of using both qualitative and quantitative approaches to self-valuation. The terminology used here (linked to research processes) helps the practitioner to see that the task of self-evaluation is not a one-off process: rather it should be viewed as an ongoing piece of school-based research, or action research. It is acknowledged that 'meaningful self evaluation has to go beyond the analysis of data and to look at the actual experience of pupils at your school' (Gross and White 2003).

In the following table, Durrant and Holden (2005) identify the range of evidence bases that already exist in schools and additional ways of collecting evidence which might be used for school self-evaluation.

Types of evidence in school-based enquiry (Durrant and Holden 2005)	
Evidence that already exists	**Additional ways of collecting evidence**
<ul><li>Pupil performance data</li><li>Minutes of meetings</li><li>Specifications (e.g. from manufacturers making claims for equipment and materials</li><li>Baseline</li><li>Policies and other documentation</li><li>Children's work</li><li>Other people's evidence – the web, reading, journals, conferences, etc.</li><li>Marking and assessment</li><li>School self-evaluation data</li><li>Professional development</li><li>documentation (e.g. performance management summaries, notes from workshops, courses, mentoring)</li></ul>	<ul><li>Records of discussion – notes, tapes, flipcharts</li><li>Observations in class, in playground, etc.</li><li>Photographs annotated by different groups</li><li>Observations of tutorial/mentoring work and follow-up conversations</li><li>Video or audio recordings (digital cameras and camcorders and be used by students to present their own perspectives)</li><li>Interviews – parents, pupils, teachers ...</li><li>Classroom journals or research diaries – paper, computer, dictaphone ...</li><li>People's relections expressed verbally, in writing (poetry, story, analogy and factual) and in pictures or diagrams</li><li>Conversations – recorded as notes</li><li>Critical incidents (analysis based on incident log)</li><li>Questionnaires, audits and surveys</li><li>Email and discussion board correspondence</li></ul>

The methods identified here combine both quantitative data and qualitative data collection. There are advantages to both but in order to develop a full picture of the school we believe it is important to ensure that there are reliable qualitative approaches built into the process. Schools are complex social settings, and to understand them the collection of data needs to reflect the unified nature of the context, rather than seeing the school as something which can be broken down into separate variables (Sherman and Webb 1988: 5)

The advantage of quantitative data is that it enables schools to see 'the big picture, the big numbers, the trends over time. (Qualitative data) ... provides the detail, the flesh on the bones and may be most valuable in pointing you towards what needs to be done' (MacBeath 1999). The challenge for many schools in gathering qualitative data is to do it in such a way that it creates a meaningful learning dialogue within the school community. Ultimately if this process is to have a significant impact on the school, it must feed back into teaching and learning and the development of the school's learning environment.

Reflective questions	Reflections/comments:
Which of the above forms of evidence are used within my school to inform self-evaluation? Is the use of it meaningful, or could it be further developed or enhanced? How?	
Who is involved in the collection and use of the different forms of evidence to inform self-evaluation within my school? Are there ways that I can become more involved in meaningful ways?	

How can schools be supported to start to explore understanding of inclusive values through effective self-evaluation?

In our experience all schools will need to engage with the language of inclusion at some point early on in the self-evaluation process. Initial discussions will probably reveal that different members of staff have different perspectives and levels of understanding related to these statements. Whilst it is important to acknowledge this and see it as an opportunity for development, it is also important not to focus on differences too much early on in this process. It seems unlikely that everyone in the school will agree about everything (Booth and Ainscow 2002) and it should never be the aim of school leaders to try and achieve this. Critical debate and informed discussion support the development of innovative practice as long as they are harnessed in a creative way; schools which become complacent about their beliefs and values can often become stagnant and stop developing (MacBeath 1999).

We have taken some key statements from the *Index for Inclusion* (Booth and Ainscow 2002), on the next page, to support practitioners in initiating such discussions within their own school community.

Inclusion in education involves

- Valuing all students and staff equally.
- Increasing the participation of students in, and reducing their exclusion from, the cultures, curricula and communities of local schools.
- Restructuring the cultures, policies and practices in schools so that they respond to the diversity of students in the locality.
- Reducing barriers to learning and participation for all students, not only those with impairments or those who are categorized as 'having special educational needs'.
- Learning from attempts to overcome barriers to the access and participation of particular students to make changes for the benefit of students more widely.
- Viewing the difference between students as resources to support learning, rather than as problems to be overcome.
- Acknowledging the right of students to an education in their locality.
- Improving schools for staff as well as for students.
- Emphasizing the role of schools in building community and developing values, as well as in increasing achievement.
- Fostering mutually sustaining relationships between schools and communities.
- Recognizing that inclusion in education is one aspect of inclusion in society.

Source: Booth and Ainscow (2002)

Practitioners may wish to utilize this list, or to develop their own school-specific questions to encourage colleagues and stakeholders within the school to start to consider:

- what they think inclusion means;
- how inclusive the school is;
- how inclusive their own classroom practice is.

Inclusive self-evaluation: creating a learning dialogue with staff, pupils and parents

Why do wider stakeholders need to be involved in meaningful self-evaluation?

Research into the development of inclusive schools (Dyson *et al.* 2002) emphasizes the importance of school culture in promoting practices which promote the participation of all students. A clear understanding and valuing of the essential principles of inclusive cultures is therefore at the heart of self-evaluation practices which utilize meaningful learning dialogues with wider stakeholders.

The Ofsted framework for inspection and the online self-evaluation form have resulted in many schools approaching the collection of qualitative data in a superficial way without considering the possibilities for rich and creative engagement with staff/pupil/parent/community voice. In many schools the response to the SEF has been to construct simplistic questionnaires for pupils and parents to be completed once a year. These questionnaires, with the addition of a school council, seem to be the limit of their aspirations; this is a missed opportunity. Whilst questionnaires are useful 'snapshots' which can give an overview of participants' responses or views, they should be viewed as the beginning of an exploration of different perspectives, not an end in themselves. Similarly, whilst the concept of a 'school council' is a valuable one, schools would be complacent were they to think that 'consultation' with this group could replace developing meaningful learning dialogue with pupils throughout the school. The role of the school council should be to add to learning dialogue, not be the only conduit for it.

However, where the SEF is seen as the outcome of inclusive self-evaluation the school will have developed a variety of ways of encouraging members of the school community to share and discuss ideas and experiences. Where this occurs, evaluation and prioritization of points for development will become more contextually specific and grounded within the actual realities and needs of the particular school community. This will enable all stakeholders to feel more involved and empowered to support whole school development.

What does the term 'learning dialogue' mean?

The very term 'learning dialogue' suggests a mutually reciprocal relationship. The idea behind learning dialogues is not that there is a pre-imposed agenda or assumptions but that, instead, a process is set up which emphasizes the joint role of evaluation and reflective thinking. The dialogue should be a learning experience for all, one to which all can equally and inclusively offer their own views and opinions. There should be no right or wrong answers, rather a mutually understood search for greater understanding of a particular issue from a variety of different perspectives. For learning dialogues to be meaningful, it is important to introduce and use them as a key approach to self-evaluation throughout the school community. In this way, all stakeholders become familiar and comfortable with the process, and will feel empowered and enabled to contribute in increasingly meaningful ways.

This is particularly important when looking for effective and appropriate ways to gain the views and opinions of pupils and parents. Developing learning dialogue is a process which, rather like inclusion, needs to be seen as an ongoing journey. We suggest that to begin the process, schools need to review their current practices and thinking. Using the following reflective questions will help with this.

Reflective questions	Reflections/comments
How does the term 'learning dialogue' relate to my own current practice? How am I enabled to feed my views and perceptions into school development/self-evaluation?	
How does it relate to the practice of my colleagues? How are they enabled to feed their views and perceptions into school development/self-evaluation?	
How are staff enabled to share in strategical planning to develop approaches to broaden our learning dialogue with pupils and parents?	
What opportunities do we currently create for pupils to share their perceptions of the school and particularly teaching and learning?	
What opportunities do we currently create for parents to share their perceptions of the school and particularly teaching and learning?	
Are there any areas which need immediate attention?	

Are there any areas we need to develop over the medium term?	
What should our long-term aims be in this area?	

The following case study illustrates the development of a learning dialogue and also the way in which inclusive self-evaluation can transform a school. Often when schools begin this kind of work, which is a form of practice-based enquiry, they start by thinking they are looking at a particular focus or area of the school. They then find that their investigation takes them into different areas. Current practice and thinking is being 'interrupted' (Ainscow 1999) and it can lead to the development of creative and innovative practice.

Case study

As a result of external pressure to raise levels of achievement through the introduction of fixed-ability groups in literacy sessions, members of staff began to engage in some school-based action research to consider how lessons encourage the participation of all students.

The research was based on a pupil voice activity called 'Hidden Voices' (Balshaw and Ainscow 1998; see Appendix 1, pp. 136–9).

Over a three-week period, the Year 2 and Year 6 teacher began introducing questions around pupil perceptions of their learning during the lesson, into plenary sessions. These would take the form of questions such as: 'How well do you think you learnt today?' 'What was helping you learn today?' 'Who was working with you today – how did you help each other with your learning?' At first pupils found these questions very new and were not sure how to respond, but with patience and gentle encouragement, discussion developed and more children began to speak and share their thoughts. Gradually a language for learning dialogue was being developed, constructed by and with the pupils. Most importantly, the students were being introduced and 'tuned-in' to the idea that they could feed back on their learning and that this could affect the way lessons would be planned in the future.

After three weeks, a morning was planned where the children were organized into mixed groups within their class, in order to discuss a number of specifically developed questions related to pupils' perceptions of groupings and the impact of various forms of support for learning. Each group had an adult to facilitate the discussion, including bilingual support, and the sessions were filmed.

Each group had a large sheet of poster paper to record their responses and at the end of each session the groups fed back to each other. The results were collated and shared among the teachers involved and the senior leadership team. The film was edited down into a short video/DVD and a staff meeting was planned in which the findings from the research activity could be shared with the rest of the staff.

The staff meeting was organized in such a way that staff members were free to engage with the evidence and respond individually and as a group. The teachers involved did not present an analysis but wanted to open up a discussion about pupil learning and groupings.

The video and discussion points were also shared with parents and governors, through a planned informal meeting – and further viewpoints and perspectives on the issues were noted.

Staff throughout the school agreed that the approach to gathering a range of different perspectives around one central key issue was crucial in enabling shared understanding of the issue and shared commitment to future planning and development work in the area. Pupils and parents were motivated and enthusiastic about contributing their ideas, and could see how their views were being considered and impacting upon whole school strategic decision making and planning.

One key outcome which staff noted was the degree to which pupils indicated that self-esteem was affected by being in a group perceived to be of a 'low ability'. The result of this was that the staff decided to make a commitment to developing flexible approaches to grouping arrangements within lessons. The short-term outcome was that pupils began to enjoy literacy lessons again, and teachers felt a stronger sense of ownership of their approaches to teaching. The long-term outcome of this was also interesting, as it led to the school beginning work on Accelerated Learning and Emotional Literacy, both of which have had a significant positive impact on the school's subsequent development.

The gathering of evidence or data for self-evaluation can be a creative and energizing process. In the case above, the school rediscovered some of its core values and was able to take ownership of the curriculum in a very powerful way. The fact that this happened in collaborative partnership with pupils, parents and governors meant that the process was much more powerful and became more sustainable. Schools need to look at areas they are concerned about or interested in developing and look for ways to work with different school groups in such a way that there is real involvement and exploration on the part of everyone involved.

How can critical friends support meaningful learning dialogues to enhance self-evaluation within the school context?

The notion of a critical friend to schools is not a new idea (Arthur and Kallick 1993; MacBeath 1999; Jones and Hennessy-Jones 2003; Swaffield 2004). However, the role of a critical friend to a school is one which has become more significant with the development of self-evaluation. Within the context of inclusive school development, Booth and Ainscow (2002: 16) define the critical friend as someone who:

- knows the school well;
- has the confidence of the school;
- is supportive but challenging.

MacBeath (1999: 110–11) adds to this list by emphasizing that the critical friend:

- seeks first to understand rather than to be understood;
- has a positive regard for the school and its community;
- is encouraging and supportive;
- helps people identify their needs and concerns;
- helps people reflect critically on their own practice;
- encourages the sharing of ideas;
- pushes for evidence;
- treats his or her own observations and judgements as one source of evidence, open to discussion and modification;
- is himself or herself open to criticism;
- is not afraid of conflict and handles it constructively;
- refers people to useful sources of information.

We highlight these features of the role, because we see the critical friend as a fundamental component in the inclusive self-evaluation process, and in developing meaningful approaches to learning dialogues which engage and include all stakeholders. Schools need a trusted 'other' who is able to support them in navigating the challenges they will encounter as they seek to develop more inclusive practices.

In 2007, following two years of piloting, the DCSF confirmed that every school would need to have a school improvement partner (SIP), appointed by the local authority (DCSF 2007a). The DCSF describe the role of the school improvement partner as providing professional challenge and support to the school, helping the school leadership to evaluate its performance, identify priorities for improvement, and plan effective change. In many respects this is not dissimilar from the role of the critical friend outlined above. However, the DCSF also see the school improvement partner as acting on behalf of the local authority and being the main channel for local authority communication about school improvement with the school. The SIP's first duty is to 'focus on pupil progress and attainment across the ability range' (DCSF 2007a: 3).

It has been suggested that the SIP can act as the school's critical friend during the self-evaluation process. Whilst there are clearly aspects of the roles which overlap, we believe that since the SIP is not independent, and instead has a duty to focus on the standards agenda and also to report to the local authority, they cannot fully meet all the requirements identified above. Because of this we recommend that schools seek to identify other professionals who can take on the role. Some schools have taken this opportunity to develop reciprocal relationships with other schools, with teachers/school leaders acting as critical friends to each other; there may also be individuals within the wider educational community who would be able to take this role on, such as education professionals in higher education. Although school governors cannot be said to be independent, there is also a useful opportunity here to develop the role of governors as critical friends. Many governing bodies struggle to find ways to engage fully with the school development process and would welcome a clearly defined strategic role whereby they could work alongside school staff in a critical but supportive way.

Concluding comments

Moving self-evaluation away from being seen as an externally imposed paper-based exercise and into a meaningful and powerful tool to enhance inclusive school development is central to the model of Inclusion of Action that we discuss through the book.

When schools are able to engage fully with the range of issues outlined here and seek to ensure greater involvement in, engagement with, and participation of all stakeholders within the prioritising of whole school development needs, they are in a much stronger position to be able to move forward with the inclusive and interlinked processes and systems that we discuss as part of the Inclusion in Action model.

Schools should be supported to consider more creative, individual and flexible ways to self-evaluate their own practices – ways which move on from being simply concerned with a narrow measure of academic progress in terms of the raising of attainment levels.

Inclusive self-evaluation supports practitioners to think more broadly about the educational realities being experienced by all involved within the school community on a day-to-day basis.

Reflective questions	Reflections/comments:
What has this chapter taught me about inclusive self evaluation?	
How does this relate to my own current practice?	

How does this relate to current strategic practice in my school?	
What are the next steps in developing more inclusive self evaluation in my school?	

3 Using Data Effectively to Identify Underachievement and Vulnerable Groups

In this chapter we critically explore the following issues and concepts:

- Meaningful data tracking
- Using data tracking systems to identify underachievement: asking the right questions
- How does the analysis of the data impact on whole school strategic development?
- Data analysis activity
- Discussion and reflection of the key issues arising from the data impacting upon whole school strategic development

Developing more inclusive practice demands that practitioners engage with a range of different forms of assessment data that are generated within the school. It is essential that staff have a clear understanding of how to use data effectively and strategically to enable meaningful change and development of current practice to occur. It is only when there is a clear link between full and rigorous scrutiny of assessment data, strengthened by professional discussion and strategic planning around the need of particular cohorts of children, that practices within the school can evolve to become more responsive to the needs of all pupils. All staff need to be fully involved in the process, and to be able to use various forms of pupil tracking records to enhance the quality of the day-to-day learning experiences of every pupil.

Where data is used well, time and priority is given within the school context to ensuring that professional discussions are planned which enable the data to come off the page, and impact upon actual practice and experiences for all pupils.

We encourage practitioners to reflect continually upon some of the more philosophical issues concerned with assessment of pupils, including:

- What is the value of assessing pupils?
- Why are we doing it?
- How are we doing it?
- Are the systems that we currently have to assess and measure pupil progress reliable and meaningful?

Meaningful data tracking

What issues relating to assessing pupil progress are dominant within current educational discourse?

It is not the intention of this chapter to look in detail at broader national issues relating to assessing and tracking pupil progress. The focus for the chapter and the book is to examine approaches to the internal school processes and systems. However, it is important first to describe briefly some of the issues, to provide a contextual basis.

Current and ongoing discussions within English education today focus on the use and value of national testing of pupils through the Standard Assessment Tests (SATs). Recently, the DCSF announced the end of formal testing at the end of Key Stage 3 and there has been an ongoing debate within education about the value of testing at the end of Key Stage 2. End of Key Stage 1 levelling is now mostly based on teacher assessment and this highlights the extent to which many educational professionals question the narrow prescriptive approaches to the measurement of achievement. However, given the current context in which Ofsted are making judgements about school effectiveness based on these measurements, schools have little choice but to engage with the DCSF/QCA-defined measurement systems.

The focus of this chapter is therefore upon the more formal aspects of assessing pupil progress and using the analysis of the data to inform whole school strategic planning. Another key aspect (which is not discussed at length but which needs to be acknowledged by the practitioner) is the need to develop effective and meaningful ongoing assessment systems, which teachers must use to directly inform their daily planning and teaching. Our work with schools which are really trying to develop this area has shown that there is a focus upon ongoing opportunities to assess prior knowledge before the teaching of new units of work. This offers the teacher the opportunity to identify which parts of any new unit of work need to be emphasized and focused upon in more detail, and which parts may already have been achieved by pupils. This enables future teaching to be carefully tailored to meet the actual needs of the particular cohort, rather than simply being based upon rigidly following a prescriptive list of content objectives.

This approach helps to ensure that teaching is matched to, and responds to, the gaps, strengths and needs of particular class cohorts, groups or individuals within the particular class group, and ensures that teaching is both relevant and focused. The focus is upon both teacher and pupils clearly understanding what the end skill and outcome of the teaching unit is, and jointly planning the steps and progression in teaching to reach that outcome.

This approach can be powerful in the planning of curriculum content, since it involves the pupils meaningfully in discussions about their current understanding and levels of ability in relation to particular curriculum content, and then uses assessment of that prior understanding to impact upon the future planned teaching. Staff may therefore also find it useful to consider ways in which assessment of prior learning impacts upon the planning and teaching of future curriculum input as well as how end of term formal assessment is used to inform whole school strategic planning mechanisms within the school.

Schools will also already be engaging with data through the use of the national systems such as Raise-Online and Making Figures Speak (DCSF 2008). It is not our intention to discuss this fully within this chapter, but it is important to draw attention to three points regarding this. Practitioners need to be aware of

- the range of valuable data and information contained within these systems;
- the need to work closely with school leaders to be able to understand the information contained within the systems;
- how to use it effectively to inform and impact upon strategic discussions and planning within the school context.

How is data currently used within schools, and who is responsible for engaging with assessment data?

We now consider the important area of internal school-based approaches and systems for assessment and data tracking. DCSF and Ofsted guidance currently strongly recommend whole school systems for monitoring pupil progress incorporating data analysis, target setting, tracking and monitoring systems. As the *Inclusion in Action* model demonstrates, this activity is seen as central to the development of inclusive whole school strategic planning to meet the needs of all, and is essential to inform the self-evaluation process.

Schools are data-rich settings, and practitioners need to ensure that they fully understand and know about the range of data that is available to them within their own particular school setting. This may include Key Stage progress data, value added data, Fischer Family Trust data, Raise-Online and school-based assessment data. Our experiences with schools have shown that data is often used in different ways by different people within the school context, and our key message is always that all staff members should have full knowledge and use of the data available in order to impact upon day-to-day practice and provision for all pupils. It is not useful, for example, if the only person who can access school performance data is the member of staff (often the administrator) who has been trained in the use of the expensive software system. This is the antithesis of what data-informed practice should be about. Teachers need to view and use data as a tool to inform their planning and provision for all their pupils.

It is useful to review the case study of schools operating at Stage 1 of the Inclusion in Action model presented earlier in Chapter 1, at the start of these discussions.

Within this system, we see a process of data tracking and analysis which lies solely within the role of one discrete staff member – the Assessment Coordinator. In schools operating at this stage of development the Assessment Coordinator plans the assessment activities, and liaises with staff members who carry out the assessments of pupils within their class. Individual staff members then give the data back to the

Stage 1

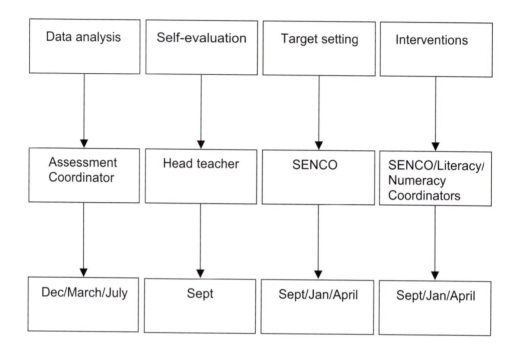

Assessment Coordinator, and have no opportunity for discussion, reflection or evaluation of the findings. Often, within a scenario such as this, the Assessment Coordinator will collate and file the information, and there will be no connection with strategic planning and evaluation to inform the development of future practices and priorities within the school.

There are clearly problems associated with an approach such as this. Although the school is fulfilling its statutory duties with respect to assessing pupil progress, there is no impact upon the ability of the school to progress further and explore ways to improve practice. There is no point in just gathering data for the sake of it. All of the systems and processes that we discuss in this book are worthwhile and valuable, and should be seen as central in any whole school improvement focus and in the ongoing evaluation and strategic planning of pupil progress and support. However, the value of the activity is undermined when it is simply seen as a paper-based activity. Instead, all staff should have a clear understanding of key principles underlying the practice of assessing pupil progress.

Before moving on to discuss this more fully it would be helpful, therefore, for the practitioner to pause and reflect upon the questions posed below to start to identify current practices in relation to assessing pupil progress within their own school context.

Reflective questions	Reflection/comments
How often is pupil progress assessed within my school context?	
How is pupil progress assessed – what assessment materials are used?	
Do these materials link in and complement end of Key Stage assessment tests (in order to ensure an accurate picture of pupil progress to be developed)?	
How is work levelled? Has there been any standardization of levelling across the whole school setting? Is levelling of work moderated within the school?	
Do all staff have a clear understanding of what progress looks like at each level – e.g. what a Level 2C piece of writing would look like?	
Is use made of the P Scales to assess pupil progress accurately before National Curriculum Level 1?	
Is there a clear understanding of what good and expected rates of progress are?	
How is the information from pupil assessment collated?	

Who is involved in this process?	
Is the information from the pupil assessments shared and discussed at a strategic level?	
How? And how does this then impact upon practice within the school?	
How are individual class and subject teachers encouraged and supported to reflect upon and evaluate cohort issues raised by the assessment data?	

The above table suggests some key questions which need to be asked of current systems and practices in assessing pupil progress. The list, however, is not exhaustive and individual schools can take the table and adapt and add to it in order to provide a useful prompt to be used within the school to review assessment procedures. Each of the key principles addressed through the reflective questions above will be taken in turn, below, with a brief critical review of the central issues behind each one. This will hopefully support practitioners to think more fully and deeply about the current systems that operate within the school system, and the overall effectiveness of each one.

By doing this, we are aiming to create 'interruptions' in practitioners' thinking (Ainscow 1999). It sometimes becomes very easy to continue to follow the same processes just because that is the way things have always been done within the school. We need to find ways to make ourselves and each other stop and think so that we can reconsider the overall effectiveness and impact of the practice.

This is often the case with data analysis and assessing pupil progress. Schools can sometimes become stuck in a particular way of assessing pupils and are unable to see the deficiencies of their particular approach, until supported by the kind of reflective questions outlined above.

Practitioners need to fully understand why they are doing things and to ensure that the systems that have been developed are meaningful and used in an ongoing and dynamic way, and that they feed into and support whole school strategic improvement and planning to improve pupil provision and outcomes for all.

For ease of discussion, the reflective questions outlined in the table above have been grouped into key areas, to enable full discussion of issues surrounding

- the practical issues associated with assessing pupil progress;
- consistent understanding of levelling across the school, and why this is important;
- analysis of the assessment data and systems to support the process.

What are the practical issues associated with assessing pupil progress?

- How often is pupil progress assessed within my school context?
- How is pupil progress assessed – what assessment materials are used?
- Do these materials link in and complement end of Key Stage assessment tests (in order to ensure an accurate picture of pupil progress to be developed)?

Pupil progress should be assessed on a regular basis within the school context, in order to be able to identify children quickly and effectively if they are underachieving, or making good progress and are therefore in need of increased levels of extension work. School staff need to carefully consider the implications and issues relating to how frequently they should formally assess pupil progress and assessment levels. These formal assessment opportunities are in addition to, and complement, the ongoing monitoring, review and evaluation of pupil progress that teachers are doing as part of their daily informal assessments. Formally assessing pupils once a year will not give school staff the information needed to make essential changes in the planning of the curriculum and in planning for further interventions and provisions during the course of the school year. By only formally assessing children's progress once a year, periods of time where children are 'stuck' and are not making adequate or effective gains in progress may be missed or not noticed.

Some schools now formally assess pupils at the end of each six – or seven-week half-term period – e.g. six times a year. The renewed frameworks from *The National Strategies* (DCSF 2008) also build in regular times during the units to assess pupil progress. Whilst this is important, we believe that it is essential that a clear balance is struck between enabling the children to actually learn, through sustained periods of well planned and enriching curriculum input, and short focused periods of formal assessment. We would argue that it is difficult to enable children to experience sustained and extended learning opportunities if the curriculum frequently needs to be interrupted for formal assessment of pupil progress.

Where we have observed systems working well, schools are assessing pupil progress on average three times a year. This process feeds in to other whole school systems and processes relating to the evaluation of pupil need and the implementation of appropriate provisions and interventions to meet those needs – as demonstrated within the Inclusion in Action model. For the assessment procedure to be effective, staff need to ensure that there is a consistent approach to assessing pupil progress followed throughout the year and across the whole school. Without this, we have seen examples of schools which have developed rigorous systems for assessing and recording pupil progress, but the data does not show trends and patterns in progress because each assessment focuses upon different skills. Staff also need to ensure that the assessment systems used throughout the year will match with end of Key Stage tests for pupils.

How can consistent understanding of attainment levels be achieved, and why is this important?

It is essential that some time is set aside for staff to come together to level and moderate each other's marked work. This helps to ensure a consistent approach to marking and levelling across the school setting, and ensures accurate understanding of skills associated with each attainment level. By setting aside some time each year to do this, schools can avoid situations where one teacher inflates assessment levels – which then impacts upon the progress seen by the next class teacher.

Staff across the school should be supported to be able to develop a clear notion of what skills are involved in achieving each level for different areas of the curriculum. Thus, staff throughout different key stages should be supported to understand what skills are expected to be demonstrated by, for example, a Level 2C writer. This helps all staff to develop knowledge about progression, previous learning and concept development. For teachers working in all key stages, it will help them to work more effectively with extension and differentiation for the full range of ability within their class group.

Current guidance from *The National Strategies* (DCSF 2008) supports developing teachers' understanding of what skills are associated with each level of ability, and advice has recently been produced to support what the DfES (2006c) and *The National Strategies* call Assessing Pupil Progress (APP). This approach recommends the detailed analysis and assessment of a small number of children operating at different levels within the class group. By utilizing this approach, it is believed that teachers will gain further understanding and in-depth knowledge of what skills are associated with different attainment levels, and be able to apply this greater understanding to the more accurate assessment of all pupils. This is a new initiative and it will be interesting to see how schools make use of it. The important principle in relation to our work with schools will be to ensure that where schools are implementing APP they are prioritizing individual needs and ensuring that staff have a clear understanding of the varying strengths and needs of each pupil. Any system is only inclusive if it puts the needs of the pupil first and not the needs of the system.

During assessments of pupil progress, it is essential that appropriate use is made of the P Scales (DCSF 2007c). The P Scales were developed in response to difficulties in tracking progress for those children operating at below Level 1. They enable small-step progress to be monitored through a number of scales from P1 to P8. Staff within schools should ensure that appropriate use is made of this resource to reflect progress – instead of simply recording WT (Working Towards), as this fails to give clear information to inform strategic planning for the needs of that individual pupil.

All teachers should have clear expectations for appropriate rates of pupil progress. The DCSF and Ofsted expect all children to make two sub-levels of progress each year (DCSF 2007d). In schools where there is good teaching and learning planned to respond to the needs of the pupils, assessment data shows that it is possible for most pupils to achieve this – when they are receiving appropriately matched support. There is, however, a wider discussion which needs to take place at national level, which relates to the validity of the DCSF definitions of progress and achievement. This issue underpins the tension that exists between the governmental push for standards and a desire to promote more inclusive school settings.

It is important that all staff discuss and have knowledge of the expectation for two sub-levels of progress each academic year, and that the progress is in relation to each child's starting point at the beginning of each academic year. When this is acknowledged, it makes the expectation seem more possible and realistic to teachers.

How can data be effectively analysed – what systems are in place to support this process?

- How is the information from pupil assessment collated?
- Who is involved in this process?
- Is the information from the pupil assessments shared and discussed at a strategic level?
- How? And how does this then impact upon practice within the school?
- How are individual class teachers encouraged and supported to reflect upon and evaluate cohort issues raised by the assessment data?

There needs to be a clearly defined system set up for the collating and recording of assessment results, in a format which supports analysis of progress over time – as well as just presenting current assessment level. Many schools make use of systems such as Assessment Manager 7, or Excel spreadsheets, to accurately record and manipulate this information. Pupil progress records which have been developed through the National Strategies Intensive Support Programme (see below) are also extremely useful. The highlighted sections illustrate nationally expected levels of attainment for each given year group.

	1C	1B	1A	2C	2B	2A	3C
Autumn							
Spring							
Summer							

The inputting of data into the assessment recording system is not something that has to be done by the practitioners themselves; often it is time-consuming and can therefore effectively be completed by office administrators. We would argue that the physical activity of actually inputting data is not the key process in ensuring staff have an understanding of the data. Rather, the important issue is to ensure that staff receive a copy of the completed assessment records and are then given structured opportunities to review and reflect the trends and patterns shown by the data. For this to be fully effective, it needs to occur at two key levels within the school:

- Strategic level;
- Class Teacher level.

Strategic level

At one level, it is essential that use is made of the assessment data by those in strategic positions within the school setting. This can be done through leadership team meetings, faculty or department meetings or year group meetings. The data needs to be objectively reviewed, to identify trends and patterns relating both to strengths and weaknesses in areas of pupil progress. However, for data analysis to be effective, it needs to go beyond the simple identification of key trends and patterns. Staff need to be supported to always consider the 'So what?' issue relating to what they have found.

For example, it is, not enough for members of the senior leadership team to identify through the assessment data a weakness in the teaching and progress of pupils in their understanding of a range of mathematical vocabulary – they then need to think about how to address this issue in order to bring about improvements. This could therefore:

- involve the need for further training of staff members in this area;
- require some rethinking about Wave 1 teaching of mathematics within those classes;
- require the allocation of further support (e.g. teaching assistants) to support the pupils to make more progress;
- require the identification of appropriate interventions which will help the children to fill in current gaps in their mathematical knowledge and then to make accelerated progress.

Class teacher level

At another level it is essential that class teachers are supported to look at the collated assessment data for their class, and to identify and reflect upon particular class-based strengths and weaknesses. Where we have seen this work well, it forms a key part of the pupil progress review meeting (see Chapter 5). The key principle is to support all staff members to move away from just collating assessment information for the sake of it, and towards an ongoing practice of collating the information, searching for key patterns and trends and then using that reflection to focus upon how they can improve and develop practice and provision to tackle any identified patterns of underachievement. Class teachers therefore need to be supported to use the analysis and reflection about the identified trends and patterns within their class to make actual and meaningful immediate changes to their teaching and planning practices, in order to support all pupils to make improvements in progress during the next school term.

Key issues which may be identified through this process may include the need for the class teacher to:

- reconsider the structure of a particular teaching input or lesson;
- provide more focus and opportunities to develop skills in a particular area;
- reconsider how he or she approaches appropriate differentiation in order to extend and challenge all pupils;
- question how support is currently used, and how to make changes in order to give further focused support to key groups of children.

Using data tracking systems to identify underachievement: asking the right questions

What questions need to be asked of assessment data?

When working with schools to analyse pupil progress, we have found that a common misconception is for attention to be focused only upon the last set of assessment data for each pupil. Thus, school leaders and class teachers can focus upon the most recent set of assessment data given in the example below – and presume that children within this Year 5 class are generally making good progress:

Assessment data: end of Year 5

Child	Reading	Writing	Numeracy
A	4C	4C	4B
B	3A	4C	4A
C	4B	4B	4B
D	4C	3A	3A
E	3B	3B	4C
F	4C	4C	4C
G	3B	3B	3A

On paper, it certainly does look as if this group of children are performing well at school. But the data presented does not tell us about progress that is being made. Instead, they tell us about attainment. Even high performing children can be underachieving and not making appropriate levels of progress, and it is therefore essential that all practitioners search beyond the current data to investigate and evaluate past progress to that point.

The table below therefore gives some extended data about the above children's progress in reading over two academic years:

Reading levels: beginning Year 4 – end Year 5

Child	Beg. Year 4	Mid. Year 4	End. Year 4	Beg. Year 5	Mid. Year 5	End. Year 5
A	3A	3B	3A	3A	3A	4C
B	2A	2A	3C	3B	3B	3A
C	3A	3A	3A	4C	4C	4B
D	3B	3A	3B	3A	3A	4C
E	2C	2B	2B	2A	3C	3B
F	4C	4B	4C	4B	4B	4B
G	2B	2B	2A	3C	3B	3B

- What does the data show?
- Are all children making effective progress?
- Are children making effective progress in relation to their ability and potential?
- What could be the possible causes of lack of progress for some of the children? What broad factors would you identify as potentially impacting upon progress?
- What questions would you start to ask about provision and curriculum for these children?

In fact, when we look again at the data to examine progress rather than exit attainment for this group of children, we notice that there is a clear pattern of underachievement. Although the exit data looks good, and the teacher or school leader could be pleased with exit levels, in fact children have been significantly underachieving. On close inspection of the data, we can notice that those children who initially we may have identified as making very good progress (Pupils F and C) have in fact made very poor rates of progress through the two school years – with Child F only moving one sub-level in two academic years. Other children who, comparably with the rest of the cohort, may initially be thought not to be making such good progress (e.g. Child E) have actually made expected progress, and have achieved four sub-levels of progress over the two academic years.

How can data be used to identify groups vulnerable to underachievement?

It is essential that all staff are supported to develop clear understanding of how to identify underachievement, using school-based assessment data systems. Underachievement is not just linked to those pupils who are operating at the lower ability levels. Underachievement can happen to any child at any time in their school career, and it is therefore important for staff to have a clear understanding of the notion of 'groups vulnerable to underachievement', or 'vulnerable groups'.

In the context of our work we have used the idea of identifying vulnerable groups of students as a way of supporting schools to understand the needs of different pupils more inclusively. National data trends indicate that there are a number of specific groups of children who are more likely to experience underachievement, or barriers to learning and participation. Statistically, the most vulnerable of these groups are

- pupils who are looked after/in local authority care.

The next most vulnerable are

- pupils with disabilities.

Other groups include:

- pupils from low-income families;
- pupils from refugee families;
- pupils from Traveller families;
- pupils whose first language is not English;
- pupils from certain minority ethnic groups.

Whilst national data sets suggest the prevalence of certain vulnerable groups, it is essential that schools do not simply use published lists to predict underachievement within their school. Instead, actual data from within the school context must be fully explored to identify school-specific groups who are experiencing barriers to learning, and who are vulnerable to underachievement. Different schools will have different lists of groups, depending on their community context.

In our work with schools, we emphasize that *every* child could potentially be vulnerable to underachievement at some point in his or her school career. Supporting practitioners to fully understand the notion of groups vulnerable to underachievement can help to open practitioners' eyes to a wider consideration of pupils who are either 'coasting' or underachieving. It is crucial that in considering vulnerable groups, schools focus on identifying and then removing the barriers to participation and achievement (Booth and Ainscow 2002). Practitioners need to think widely about groups vulnerable to underachievement, and to use understanding of this notion to impact upon how they ask critical and challenging questions about assessment data, using the answers to directly inform future teaching, planning and strategic decision making. Staff should be supported to use their understanding of vulnerable groups to look for patterns of underachievement within particular vulnerable groups specific to their class group.

Is there a difference between SEN and underachievement?

Practitioners should be clear that there is a difference between underachievement and SEN. Even when specific learning needs have been identified for a pupil, it is possible for that child to be operating at lower levels of ability than age-related expectations but yet to be making progress and not underachieving in relation to progress against baseline starting points. Where pupils with SEN are supported in a positive and inclusive setting, where targets and learning experiences are planned to respond to their individual needs, they are able to make accelerated progress.

Similarly, as the discussions about groups vulnerable to underachievement above demonstrate, it is possible for other pupils (including those children who are middle ability – with no identified area of need) or those pupils who have been identified as gifted and talented potentially to underachieve.

It is therefore essential that the practitioner is supported to use careful scrutiny of the assessment data to identify underachievement – rather than relying on rather stereotypical notions and preconceived assumptions about which pupils may potentially underachieve.

How does the analysis of the data impact on whole school strategic development?

The effective analysis of data should lead to meaningful change and improvement within the school setting. It is of fundamental importance that schools ask searching questions of their pupil progress data. Behind each set of assessments lies an individual child's story and it is the task of school leaders to look beyond the numbers and identify exactly why a particular student is not making progress in certain areas. In this way schools can begin to identify and remove the barriers to student achievement and participation in all aspects of school life.

Using the information shared in the previous sections of the chapter, it is now important to consider and give examples of how practitioners can use this information and understanding to impact upon whole school strategic development. We are going to illustrate the process through the use of a direct example which can be worked through at two different levels.

1   As an individual exercise in thinking objectively about data with which you are not involved personally.
2   As a whole staff INSET activity to promote discussion, reflection and understanding of the key principles and issues which can then be related to individual school practice.

Data analysis activity

Look at the data presented below for two classes: Class A and Class B.

For each class, two sets of assessment data for different subjects are provided as well as a class Profile of Need to provide further information about the context and profile of needs within the class as a whole (see Chapter 4 for more information about class Profiles of Need).

As you look at the information presented for each class, start to reflect critically and analyse any key patterns or trends that you can identify. Then go beyond the identification of trends to the most important part of strategic analysis of data, which is the focus upon 'So what?'

- So what needs to happen?
- So what does this tell us about current provision and practice?
- So what action can we take to make improvements in this area?

Try considering the following questions:

- What does the data tell you about the key issues and patterns of achievement or underachievement within each class?
- What might be possible causes for these trends?
- So what needs to happen now to start to develop some of the identified issues and areas of underachievement?
- So what implication has this for provision and practice?

The remaining discussions in this chapter will also be based upon this data activity, and it will be used to emphasize some of the key issues in relation to how effective data analysis can impact upon whole school strategic planning.

Activity

Key for needs identified in class Profile of Needs

SA   School Action
SA+   School Action Plus
ST   Statement of SEN
G&T Gifted and talented
EAL English as an additional language
LAC Looked after child
SS   Social services involvement
TRA Traveller
YC   Young carer

Class A Profile of Need

Pupil	Needs
Amir	
Shakil	**EAL; G&T**
Haroun	**SA** Cognition and Learning
Phoun	
Omar	
Charlotte	
Jacob	
Joshua	**SS**
Shahmima	
Peter	**SA+** Specific learning difficulties
Helen	
Lili	
Phillip	
George	**SA** Behaviour, emotional and social Difficulties
Dawit	
Mei	
Ani	
Maggie	**G&T**
Sally	**SA** Cognition and learning
Paul	
Onjana	**SA** Cognition and learning
Samuel	
Joe	

Class A Pupil tracking: Year 3 reading

Pupil	July 07	Dec 07	March 08	July 08	Dec 08
Amir	2C	2B	2B	2B	2B
Shakil	1B	1A	1A	2C	2A
Haroun	P7	1C	1C	1B	1A
Phoun	2C	2B	2B	2C	2B
Omar	2C	2C	2C	2B	2A
Charlotte	2C	2C	2B	2B	2B
Jacob	1C	1B	1B	1A	2C
Joshua	2C	2B	2B	2C	2C
Shahmima	1A	1A	2C	2B	2B
Peter	P6	P7	P8	1C	1C
Helen	1A	2C	2B	2B	2B
Lili	1B	1A	1A	1A	2C
Phillip	1C	1B	1A	1A	2C
George	1A	2C	2B	2C	2B
Dawit	1A	2C	2C	2C	2C
Mei	1B	1A	2C	2B	2B
Ani	1A	1A	2C	2C	2B
Maggie	1A	2C	2C	2B	3C
Sally	1C	1B	1B	1A	2C
Paul	2C	2C	2B	2B	2B
Onjana	P7	P8	1C	1B	1A
Samuel	1B	1A	2C	2C	2B
Joe	1A	1A	1A	2C	2B

Class A Pupil tracking: Year 3 writing

Pupil	July 07	Dec 07	March 08	July 08	Dec 08
Amir	1C	1B	1A	1A	1A
Shakil	1B	1A	1A	1B	1A
Haroun	P7	1C	1C	1B	1A
Phoun	1B	1A	2C	2C	2C
Omar	2C	2C	2B	2B	2A
Charlotte	2C	2C	2B	2B	2A
Jacob	1C	1B	1B	1A	1A
Joshua	2C	2B	2B	2C	2C
Shahmima	1A	1A	2C	2B	2B
Peter	P6	P7	P8	1C	1C
Helen	1A	2C	2B	2B	2B
Lili	1B	1A	1A	1A	2C
Phillip	1C	1B	1A	1A	1A
George	1A	2C	2C	2C	2C
Dawit	1A	2C	2C	2C	2C
Mei	1B	1A	2C	2B	2B
Ani	1A	1A	2C	2C	2B
Maggie	1A	2C	2C	2B	3C
Sally	1C	1B	1B	1A	2C
Paul	1C	1C	1A	1A	2C
Onjana	P7	P8	1C	1B	1A
Samuel	1B	1A	2C	2C	2B
Joe	1A	1A	1A	2C	2C

Class B Profile of Need

Pupil	Needs
Amina	**SA** Behaviour, emotional and social difficulties
Shahan	**SA** Cognition and learning
Harry	**SS**
Fon	
Ollie	**SA** Behaviour, emotional and social difficulties; **SS**
Charlie	**G&T**
Jamilla	
Jonah	**SA+** Autistic spectrum difficulties **G&T** Numeracy
Shahana	**LAC**
Ping	**SA** Behaviour, emotional and social difficulties
Gloria	**SA** Cognition and learning; emotional
Lily	**SS**
Terry	
Alamen	**EAL**
Mandy	**G&T**
Nadvee	Communication and interaction
Lifa	
Meg	**SA** Behaviour, emotional and social difficulties
Eloise	**SA** Cognition and learning
Jennifer	
Nicola	Behaviour, emotional and social difficulties
Milo	**SA+** Behaviour, emotional and social difficulties
Leo	

Class B Pupil tracking: Year 8 writing

Pupil	July 07	Dec 07	March 08	July 08	Dec 08
Amina	3A	3B	3A	3A	4C
Shahan	3C	3C	3B	3A	4C
Harry	4B	4B	4A	4B	4A
Fon	3A	4C	4C	4C	4B
Ollie	4B	4C	4B	4C	4C
Charlie	4A	4A	4A	5C	5C
Jamilla	3B	3B	3A	4C	4B
Jonah	3B	3B	3B	4C	4C
Shahana	3A	4C	4B	4A	5C
Ping	4C	4B	4B	4A	4B
Gloria	3B	3A	4C	4C	4C
Lily	3A	4C	4B	4C	4A
Terry	4C	4B	4A	4A	4A
Alamen	2C	2C	3B	4C	4A
Mandy	5C	5C	5C	5C	5C
Nadvee	3C	3C	3B	3B	3A
Lifa	4C	4B	4B	4A	5C
Meg	4C	4A	5C	4A	4A
Eloise	3C	3B	3B	4C	4C
Jennifer	3B	3A	4B	4A	4A
Nicola	3B	3A	3A	4C	4B
Milo	3B	3A	3A	4C	4B
Leo	3A	4C	4C	4B	4A

Class B Pupil tracking: Year 8 numeracy

Pupil	July 07	Dec 07	March 08	July 08	Dec 08
Amina	4C	4B	4A	4A	5C
Shahan	3C	3C	3B	3A	4C
Harry	3A	4C	4C	4B	4A
Fon	4C	4B	4A	5C	5B
Ollie	4B	4C	4B	4C	4C
Charlie	5B	5B	5A	5A	5A
Jamilla	4B	4B	4A	5C	5B
Jonah	5B	5B	5B	5A	5A
Shahana	3A	4C	4B	5C	5B
Ping	4C	4B	4A	4A	5C
Gloria	3B	3A	4C	4C	4B
Lily	3A	4C	4B	4A	4A
Terry	4C	4B	4A	5C	5C
Alamen	2C	3B	3A	4B	5C
Mandy	5B	5B	5B	5B	5A
Nadvee	4C	4B	4B	4B	4A
Lifa	4C	4B	4B	4A	5C
Meg	4C	4A	5C	4A	5C
Eloise	3C	3B	3B	4C	4C
Jennifer	3B	3A	4B	4A	4A
Nicola	4B	4A	5C	5B	5C
Milo	4C	4C	4B	4B	4A
Leo	3A	4C	4C	4B	4A

Discussion and reflection of the key issues arising from the data impacting upon whole school strategic development

Key issues

Class A	Class B
• Middle ability children underachieving consistently	• A high number of children with specific needs
• Children with cognition and learning SEN are making good progress	• Many children with specified difficulties with behaviour
• Boys' writing is an issue	• Over-balance of boys within the class group as a whole
	• Numeracy an area of strength
	• Some vulnerable groups making good progress

The table above is not exhaustive, and practitioners may have identified other key issues; however, the focus throughout is upon moving forward from the identification of the key issues, so a few are highlighted to discuss as an example of the process involved.

Our experiences suggest that schools often stop at the stage of identifying key issues. They may use the assessment data to identify the key trends and patterns, but then neglect the next critical phase – that of rigorous critical and reflective thinking about the issues. Why are these occurring and what more needs to be done to address them within the school setting?

Within the data example given above, data from Class A indicates that middle ability children are underachieving. At a strategic level, this would suggest that there needs to be further focus upon provision both at Wave 1 and 2 within this class. Further training may need to be identified and provided to support the teacher and any teaching assistants working with the class to consider appropriate Wave 2 interventions that may be able to give these middle ability children a boost to accelerate their progress. Leaders within the school should also compare this trend with trends and patterns within other classes to identify whether this is a whole-school issue – thereby requiring a whole school priority focus, possibly through the school development plan; or a class teacher-specific issue – indicating an individual continuing professional development (CPD) training need.

The data also show that within Class A, children identified with cognition and learning SEN are making good progress. At a strategic level this can be highlighted and used as an opportunity to scrutinize interventions and patterns of support that are working well and enabling the pupils to make good or accelerated rates of progress. The information gathered can be shared with staff across the school in order to enhance the effectiveness of interventions and support within other classes. It can also be used to inform strategic decisions in the future about which approach to take to meeting needs.

The Profile of Need within Class B is very high, with many children having a diverse range of needs which may impact upon their learning. Just from this information alone, leaders within the school should be able to make strategic decisions and judgements about staffing and support levels needed to manage this class group, both within teaching lessons and as they move around the school.

The Profile of Need indicates that there is a high number of children identified with specific behaviour difficulties. This will directly impact upon the type of teaching approach the class as a whole will need and, at a strategic level, leaders should be reflecting upon the training and support needs for staff working within this class group. Careful analysis of systems in place at Wave 1 to meet the behaviour needs of this class will be needed.

The data from Class B indicate that progress within numeracy is good, and that this is therefore an area of strength within the class. Leaders within the school should consider reasons for this good progress, which may reflect the pupils' preferred learning style but may also indicate good or excellent subject teaching in this area. Again, information and analysis of the underlying factors for this good progress can be shared with others across the school, in order to impact upon and develop practice throughout the school setting.

The data from Class B also show that there is an inconsistent pattern of achievement across different vulnerable groups. Some (such as those with English as an additional language (EAL) and looked after children (LAC)) are making good progress – and reflective questions need to be asked about what is the underlying cause of this progress. What has been put in place to enable those children to make such good progress, and can this be replicated with others across the school? Other vulnerable groups, including gifted and talented pupils, are underachieving – and again the reasons behind this need to be interrogated. Leaders within the school need to consider how the needs of gifted and talented pupils are being addressed and met, and whether further support and provision needs to be put in place to support the children to make accelerated progress.

Concluding comments

Pupil tracking and data analysis are powerful tools in supporting more in-depth understanding of the needs of specific cohorts and individual children. It is essential that school staff are supported to be able to use data systems meaningfully as a starting point for scrutinizing pupil participation and achievement. Through rigorous reflection and discussion about the issues found within the data, staff should work together strategically to plan next steps in developing more inclusive and enabling learning experiences to respond to the needs of every pupil.

This is a key part of the Inclusion in Action model, and staff should be supported to move the analytical and reflective scrutiny of assessment data forward into action, by interlinking data analysis meaningfully with planning and thinking about interventions, provision mapping and target setting.

Practitioners can use the following reflective questions as starting points for reviewing their own practice.

Reflective questions	Reflections/comments
What has this chapter taught me about inclusive data analysis?	

How does this relate to my own current practice?	
How does this relate to current strategic practice in my school?	
What are the next steps in developing more inclusive data analysis in my school?	

4 Inclusive Interventions

In this chapter we critically explore the following issues and concepts:

- Planning interventions
- The Waves of Intervention: adapting and developing the National Strategies model according to school context
- Monitoring and evaluating impact: what's working in the school?

Planning a range of appropriate and meaningful interventions in a strategic way to respond to the needs of individuals, cohorts and whole schools is an essential task within the whole school development cycle.

Central to the notion of inclusive interventions that we discuss here is a firm acknowledgement of the importance of high-quality Wave 1 teaching which responds fully to the needs of the particular cohort. Teachers need to reflect upon their own practice in such a way that they are actively identifying pedagogical barriers to participation and achievement for all pupils.

Interventions are any form of teaching and learning that has been specially tailored to meet the needs of individuals or specific groups of pupils. They should not reinforce segregationary practices. Rather, practitioners need to understand that all pupils should have equal access to their classroom learning environment, and that appropriate and effective interventions can be delivered within and through classroom teaching. In our view an inclusive school encourages a range of activities and groupings in which all children participate.

This part of the Inclusion in Action model interlinks with and builds upon the rigorous scrutiny and reflection of current assessment data (discussed in Chapter 3). Where this happens as part of the dynamic model, teachers can effectively identify where interventions may be needed and review their teaching practices in relation to the specific needs of different cohorts.

Planning interventions

What is meant by the term 'intervention', and how has understanding and use of the term changed?

The need for schools to identify underachievement and to address this through the effective use of intervention programmes is a major feature of current guidance coming from the DCSF, the Primary and Secondary Strategies and Ofsted. Whilst the terminology used is therefore commonplace throughout educational discussions, this is not to say that it is unproblematic.

Indeed, whilst the notion of 'intervention' is not new, it should be acknowledged that the term can still mean different things to different people. Traditionally, intervention could be viewed as a specialized form of support, often identified and given to those children with high or complex levels of SEN. Children would be identified with a given need – for example poor speech and language skills or difficulty in phonological processing – and a specialized programme may have been given to them to help to address the need. Historically, this may have been given through withdrawn 1:1 support, and often, once the need and programme had been identified, there was little impetus to review and update it.

In England the roots of this approach to 'support' for individual pupils lie within the Warnock report (Warnock 1978), which introduced the concept of special educational need and the notion of statements of special educational need. Identifying students with disabilities or special educational needs and providing specified support for them was reinforced by the SEN Code of Practice in 1993 (DfEE 1993) and the revised SEN Code of Practice in 2001 (DfES 2001). Although the Warnock report and both codes have provided a structure and much needed guidance for professionals in supporting students with special educational needs they have also led to the development of a non-inclusive culture in many English schools. This is because schools have tended to adopt a medical model in considering the best way to support students that they have identified. By identifying the deficit and providing support to 'counter' this, schools were able to ignore the exclusionary barriers to participation and achievement which they were creating systemically for many students. Additionally, the support that was provided for students with special educational needs was often ineffective and not monitored with any rigour or analysis of impact (Gross and White 2003; DCSF 2007d).

Since the introduction of the National Strategies, intervention has started to be viewed in a broader sense, and national intervention programmes, such as the 'Additional Literacy Support' (ALS), 'SpringBoard Numeracy' programme and, at secondary level, 'Developing Readers' have been introduced. This has helped schools and practitioners to start to think of interventions in a less specialized way, and start to consider the need for large groups of children to access further support through structured intervention programmes in order to make effective progress.

Intervention needs to be considered in its broadest sense. It is not just about a 1:1 programme for a child with complex and high levels of need; it is also not about a standard 'package' intervention programme delivered to whole groups of children in the same way, just because they fit the criteria of age or level of ability. Intervention is about ensuring that the needs of all pupils are met in the most appropriate and relevant way. Sometimes this can be through the delivery of a standardized national intervention programme, such as the Early Literacy Support programme – but often it means identifying the real needs of the child or group of children and ensuring that the materials are adapted to suit their particular needs.

How can the potential benefits of early intervention be explored within the school context?

Early intervention is crucial in planning effective support for all pupils, and a key part of the role of senior leaders within the school will therefore be identifying and analysing trends and patterns of underachievement within the school and thinking creatively about ways to address these from the earliest possible time. Where this works well, schools have analysed the intake from their catchment area and the particular and individual needs of children on arrival at school, and have used this information to plan effective support and intervention from children's entry into school, rather than waiting until increased levels of difficulty become apparent (see case studies below).

Case study

Staff within a small rural primary school had noticed patterns of skill level on entry to school at age 4 change over a number of years. During analysis of data emerging from the Foundation Stage it was noted that the entry speech, language and communication skills were significantly lower than in previous years.

Staff within the school discussed possible reasons for this, and also looked critically at the impact of the trend upon attainment throughout the Foundation Stage and the children's ability to access the learning environment effectively upon arrival within the school setting.

The Foundation Stage leader also made links with local nursery and pre-school environments to talk about the trends, to see whether this was a growing pattern and how the pre-school settings were having to adapt their approach to cater for this change.

Staff noted that support and provision needed to be put in place in the Foundation Stage, as early intervention. Waiting to deal with the issues later, when children became older and the difficulties more apparent, might have led to additional challenges in accessing the curriculum and associated self-esteem or behaviour difficulties.

As a result of the discussions, the school identified that it was essential for them to critically review and change the way that they planned and provided for children within the Foundation Stage.

Speech and language screening was implemented to screen all the children and to identify individual, group and whole cohort needs with speech and language skills. Using this information, whole-class, small group and 1:1 interventions and strategies were planned and delivered.

Secondary case study

Within the secondary context, one school identified difficulties with their new Year 7 cohort. The cohort had been drawn from a number of different feeder primary schools and included a number of children with significant social, emotional and behavioural difficulties. Early in Year 7, the teachers noted that the new cohort was finding it extremely difficult to form positive relationships with each other – and there had already been small outbreaks of unacceptable aggressive behaviour between pupils.

Staff decided that the situation would not improve without focused planning and action from the staff themselves, and that to leave the problem and 'hope that it would go away' would just serve to make the issue more of a problem further up the school.

The school therefore liaised closely with key members of Specialist Teaching Services' and outside professionals to look at creative ways to work proactively and positively with this cohort to encourage the children to start to mix appropriately.

A number of strategies were suggested, ranging from simple class-based and playground-based strategies and support to more innovative and high-impacting strategies involving team building days and extended residential visits.

By the end of the year, as a result of the focused support, planning and reflection that the staff had put in to meeting this cohort's social, emotional and behavioural needs, the cohort as a whole were much more settled and at ease with each other. Behaviour within the classroom and around the school had improved vastly, and the pupils themselves were demonstrating the ability to make good choices about friendships and peer relationships.

As a result of the support, the cohort became one of the most close and supportive year groups in the school. The pupils were able to demonstrate improved social skills, which impacted upon learning skills and the ability for them to concentrate and make progress within curriculum areas.

Staff at the school decided to monitor the impact and effectiveness of the approach continually and, as a result of noting such positive developments, decided to continue to use and adapt many of the strategies and approaches for general use with all new Year 7 cohorts entering the school. This helped staff to understand the difficulties that many Year 7 pupils experience in forming new relationships with peers from a range of different school settings and to set up a system to support the pupils positively and proactively through the transition period.

It was agreed that early intervention actually reduced the need for extreme measures to be used later on – and that exclusions within the school, and particularly in Year 7, were significantly reduced as a result.

What historical models or approaches exist relating to how interventions are planned within the school context and what are the disadvantages of these approaches for effective strategic planning?

When planning specific intervention it is essential for schools to move away from the old 'resource and hope' model – where resources are put in and then staff 'hope' that they will have some sort of impact. This has often been the case with the introduction of teaching assistants to provide further support. Research suggests that there is no evidence to prove that just by putting further teaching assistant support into a class there will be any impact upon standards and attainment (Gross & White, 2003). Rather, the evidence demonstrates that careful planning for the specific use of that additional adult is required in order for it to have a beneficial effect.

Schools are also encouraged to move away from a 'lifestyle' model of intervention. In this model individual needs are carefully identified, and this then leads to an intervention being developed and used as a 'lifestyle' to support the child, without being regularly reviewed, evaluated and adapted. For example, where a child has been identified as having a significant problem with phonics on entry into the school context, we have seen schools use this 'label of need' to continually deliver the same programme of support to the child year after year, without actually monitoring its effectiveness or it age-appropriateness.

How can schools plan interventions more effectively?

Schools must ensure that the specific needs of the child at each stage of his or her school career are identified and addressed, through rigorous monitoring of progress and analysis of continuing areas of difficulty. By engaging in this process, school staff can ensure that small-step, time-limited interventions can be set up which are appropriate to the child's stage of conceptual development and also age-appropriate. At the end of each time-limited period, the progress made through the intervention will be analysed and monitored, and the next small-step intervention relevant to the child's individual needs can be planned. In this way, the intervention becomes less like a 'lifestyle' for the child – and more like focused specific support which is continuously planned to help the child to move forward to the next phase of learning.

Reflective questions	Reflection/comment
How is the term intervention used within my school context?	

Are issues around early intervention considered within my school context? How am I involved in strategic thinking and planning for early intervention within my school? Can my role in this be enhanced? How? What examples are there of early interventions? How successful are they? What has been the benefit for pupil progress through the whole school? Are there other whole school needs which may be appropriately addressed through meaningful early intervention?	
Are there any examples within my school context of the 'resource and hope' or 'lifestyle' models of intervention? How could practice be moved forward to enable more strategic approaches to intervention planning?	
How are small-step, time-limited, planned interventions used within my school setting? How is progress reviewed and monitored through the intervention? How does this evaluation and analysis of progress impact upon planning of next-step interventions for individuals or groups?	

The Waves of Intervention: adapting and developing the National Strategies model according to school context

What are the Waves of Intervention?

For some time, the Primary National Strategy in England (DfES 2002) has promoted a model for supporting all children – using the Waves of Intervention.

> ### The National Literacy Strategy (NLS) and National Numeracy Strategy (NNS) assume three 'waves' of support for children
>
> The SEN Code of Practice (DfES, 2001) describes a 'graduated response' to identifying and meeting special educational needs which may be mapped onto the NLS/NNS three waves as follows:
>
> **Wave 1** The effective inclusion of all children in a high-quality literacy hour and daily mathematics lesson ('quality first teaching').
>
> Children may be at any point on the 'graduated response' – that is, the usual differentiated curriculum, *School Action* or *School Action Plus*.
>
> **Wave 2** Small-group intervention (NNS Springboard, NLS Early Literacy Support, Additional Literacy Support and Further Literacy Support programmes, booster classes, equivalent LEA or school-based programmes) for children who can be expected to 'catch up' with their peers as a result of the intervention – that is, who do not have special educational needs related specifically to learning difficulties in literacy or mathematics. Wave 2 interventions are not primarily SEN interventions. Where intervention programmes are delivered without modification within the designated year group, there is no requirement that the children involved should be placed on *School Action*.
>
> Children included in Wave 2 interventions may on occasion already be at *School Action* or *School Action Plus*. This will be where they have special educational needs such as emotional and behavioural difficulties, communication and interaction difficulties, or sensory or physical impairment, for which they are receiving other forms of support.
>
> **Wave 3** Specific targeted approaches for individual children identified as requiring SEN intervention. Children at Wave 3 may have particular needs related specifically to mathematics or literacy, or needs associated with other barriers to their learning. Provision at Wave 3 is likely to draw on specialist advice.
>
> It may involve the adjustment of learning objectives and teaching styles, and/or individual support. It aims to reduce gaps in attainment and facilitate greater access to Waves 1 or 2.
>
> (DfES 2002:)

This concept and model of working has also been incorporated into the Secondary National Strategy (DfES 2003), with the introduction of the move towards setting up Intervention Teams to evaluate and monitor the impact of appropriate intervention programmes. This has been followed by the introduction of the 'Renewing Intervention' websites, which reinvigorate the idea of setting up School Intervention Teams, but also support this with useful training and resource materials:

www.standards.dfes.gov.uk/intervention

www.standards.dfes.gov.uk/progressionmaps/

www.standards.dfes.gov.uk/local/ePDs/leading_on_intervention/site/u1/index.htm

Undoubtedly, the Waves of Intervention approach can prove a powerful tool in developing inclusive whole school improvement strategies. However, practitioner evidence suggests that in order for it to be fully effective, schools should first ensure that all staff have a clear understanding of this Waved Model and, then, find ways to adapt and extend the approach so that it impacts upon all whole school systems.

Ofsted in England have argued that schools need to improve the use and effectiveness of a range of interventions within the school context. Ofsted (2004a) found that:

- there is still limited knowledge of the management of the three Waves of intervention;
- there is a lack of rigour in the use of school-based assessment data. Pupil tracking systems need to be improved;
- the causes of underachievement are not often identified or remedied early enough;
- there is a lack of understanding of a wide range of effective interventions – often interventions are used as a catch-all rather than for targeted support;
- schools need to monitor the quality of interventions and their impact on pupil outcomes.

How can thinking about the Waves of Intervention be extended to promote more inclusive approaches to teaching and learning?

Since 2002, understanding of the practical possibilities of applying the Waves of Intervention throughout whole school systems has developed. Innovative and creative schools have extended this original idea into a more inclusive model of whole school development (see case studies).

We would argue that in order to maximize the benefits of this waved model for whole school improvement, it should not be viewed in narrow terms. In the past, many schools have seen it only as something applicable to literacy or numeracy. Some schools, however, in the last few years have creatively extended this notion, and have applied the idea of a waved response to interventions to other aspects of whole school development including:

- personal, social and emotional development;

- the Every Child Matters agenda;
- the creative curriculum;
- basic skills development.
- whole class teaching and learning approaches.

Indeed, some schools have successfully incorporated aspects of several of the above points in order to produce a waved model of support and interventions which appropriately matches the priorities and needs of their particular school context, and which can clearly link with and enhance the provision mapping processes – see case study below.

Case study: Developing the notion of a waved model of interventions to respond to the complexities of the individual school context

The Literacy Coordinator/Head of the English Department first found out about the Waves of Intervention during a National Literacy Strategy training session.

The session focused upon particular interventions that would be useful to raise attainment in reading and writing, relating to the three waves.

The Literacy Coordinator/Head of the English Department returned to his school setting and continued to reflect upon the idea, as he had been aware for some time that a more planned response to coordinating support for particular groups of children was needed within the school.

This was discussed with the SENCO. Both agreed that this model provided the framework for thinking that was missing within the school at that time.

These thoughts were shared and discussed with the senior leadership team. The discussions quickly became exciting as different members of the team thought about how the model could be adapted to respond to their different areas of responsibility.

As a result of that meeting a decision was made to share the waved model of interventions with the rest of the staff, but that the model would be extended to enable it to incorporate various aspects of school development.

As a whole staff the Waves of Intervention were discussed during a series of staff meetings. The training started with input around the notion that had been put forward during the National Literacy Strategy training session. Further sessions started to consider other whole school priorities which could be included. The staff meeting sessions became invaluable. As a large staff, it enabled shared thinking and discussion from a range of different perspectives, and enabled a more committed and shared approach to be adopted throughout all teaching and support staff.

Over time, the staff as a whole came up with an adapted model which matched the particular needs of the school, and which everyone had had some input in developing. Staff were excited about the model and enthusiastic about using it to support the children more flexibly and creatively.

> The original model focused upon interventions to develop basic skills and also interventions to meet the children's range of personal social and emotional needs.
>
> Over time, the model that developed continued to be discussed, and it has since evolved and changed in response to different priorities.
>
> The model was shared with outside professionals and consultants, including an educational psychologist, a local authority adviser, a primary strategy consultant and the school improvement partner.
>
> As a result of these discussions, the model now effectively incorporates aspects of the five strands from the Every Child Matters agenda. This helps staff to continue to focus on these in a meaningful and relevant way, and helps to plan interventions in a more focused manner.

The English National Strategies originally linked the Waves of Intervention with the graduated levels of the SEN Code of Practice (School Action, School Action Plus and Statemented). This restricts and narrows the usefulness of the concept as a whole school improvement tool. Indeed, the limitations of the approach proposed by the English National Strategies are that, contrary to its intentions, it has its roots in an SEN-deficit model and that this can lead to exclusionary practices rather than developing inclusive education for all.

Reflective practitioners who are trying to develop more inclusive practices are beginning to engage in a much more flexible and meaningful way with the model, and are extending its use to ensure that it provides an effective and inclusive model for whole school development. We argue that the Waves of Intervention model should no longer be seen as an SEN-based model, but as an inclusive model helping schools to ensure that all children are able to participate and make appropriate progress in relation to their particular skills, strengths and needs. Individual schools should be encouraged to reflect upon the context of their school, and particular cohorts of children, and to utilize the waved model of interventions to support the children within that cohort. Schools are finding, through an in-depth analysis of the needs of individual cohorts, that it is not always just children with learning difficulties and disabilities that require focused support or long-term intervention. At times, depending upon the particular cohort, it may be children from other vulnerable groups such as EAL (English as an additional language) or gifted and talented pupils, who require intensive and specialist Wave 3 provision to meet their needs – see case study below.

Case study

The SENCO started using the Waves of Intervention to track the programmes that he had in place to support children at School Action, School Action Plus and children with statements of special educational need upon the school SEN register. Very quickly, however, he realized through the termly analysis of school-based assessment data that actually the children on the SEN register were making good progress in relation to their baseline skill levels and as a result of the input and support that was being put in place.

The SENCO identified that whilst high-quality SEN practice was embedded within teaching and practice throughout the school, other children, particularly those who were gifted and talented, did not seem to be fulfilling their potential.

The SENCO therefore decided to extend the initial model of Waves of Intervention to incorporate a range of interventions and support programmes to meet the needs of all the vulnerable groups within the school. Staff identified particular support and interventions that was put in place at Wave 1, 2 and 3 to meet the diverse needs of children with English as an additional language, gifted and talented children and Traveller children.

As a result of this extended planning, the needs of children throughout the school are being effectively identified, and intervention programmes are being implemented to meet the needs of all children – not just those on the SEN register.

In order for the model of Waves of Intervention to become effective within a school, time needs to be devoted to ensure shared understanding of and commitment to the model. This needs to be achieved through reflective and collaborative professional discussions and the sharing of examples of good practice.

Only when all staff members are on board and fully understand the issues being addressed will whole school inclusive practice be able to move forward. As staff engage in this way of looking critically at what provision and support is in place across the school at each wave, discussions can start to identify school-specific strengths, and also gaps in provision and support. The following section therefore contains clear information about each Wave of Intervention, and raises critical questions and issues which can be considered and addressed within staff groups.

What is Wave 1 intervention?

Wave 1 is the absolute foundation for building and developing good-quality inclusive practice within the school, and it is therefore essential that staff invest time in fully scrutinizing what is happening at Wave 1 within their classroom or across the whole school. School staff should view intervention and support through the waves as a pyramid model, with Wave 1 at the bottom and Wave 3 at the top:

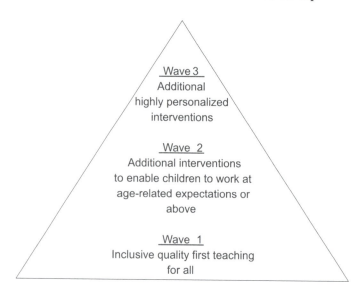

School staff need to understand that Wave 1 is central to any discussion about achievement, attainment and progress within the school setting. Wave 1 focuses upon good-quality inclusive teaching to meet the needs of *all* pupils within a given cohort. The intention is that 80 per cent of all children within that given cohort will be able to access the learning and make progress through the support offered at Wave 1.

This is significant, and when schools scrutinize and analyse pupil progress within that cohort, if 80 per cent have not made progress this does not mean that the school need to put in further intensive withdrawn intervention programmes. Rather, staff should recognize that it identifies that what is being provided at Wave 1 is not appropriate to the needs of the children of that cohort, and that fundamental changes need to be made to the teaching provided for all.

This is not to say that this is always due to poor teaching – in our experience we have seen some outstanding teachers not making expected progress with particular cohorts of children. When we critically review the issues associated with this, it becomes apparent that although the teaching is of very high calibre, the teaching style or approach does not fully match the learning style of the learners within that particular class cohort.

It is therefore essential that any review of provision and intervention starts with identifying what are the particular needs of the cohort with which we are working.

Only by doing this, and by developing a clear picture of the learning and social, emotional and behavioural needs of the class can teachers ensure that they appropriately match their Wave 1 teaching style to the needs of their particular class.

Indeed, it has been our experience that in many schools the practice is more like an upturned pyramid, with little time and energy being put in to critically review practice at Wave 1, and with more and more time being put in to add additional and intensive, withdrawn interventions at Wave 3. The outcome of this approach is that staff can feel stressed and stretched, with class teachers calling for more and more additional resources to meet additional need, without considering the impact of the focus of their whole-class teaching approach.

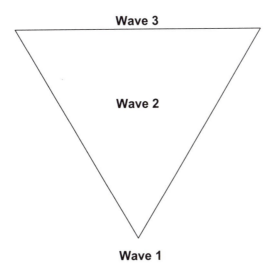

How can we use knowledge of the needs of specific cohorts of children to enhance provision at Wave 1?

In our work with schools we have found that staff have found it useful to regularly complete a simple class Profile of Need, and to use this to plan directly for the support that is needed to manage the diverse and particular needs of the cohort through appropriate Wave 1 planning. This has been an extremely valuable tool for teachers within primary schools to ensure that they have up-to-date and relevant information about the individual children that they work with every day. It has, however, also been an extremely useful and effective tool to develop within the secondary school, where teachers are working with very large numbers of different children within different teaching groups. The class Profiles of Need offer a simple tool for drawing together a range of information which secondary school teachers can then efficiently utilize to inform their planning.

Using a very simple format which, at its basic level, can simply be a copy of the class register, teachers indicate next to each child any particular needs or vulnerable groups that that child may fall into. The 'labels' or vulnerable groups that are identified will be school – and cohort-specific, but the following basic categories may provide a useful starting point:

SA	School Action	SA+	School Action Plus
ST	Statement of SEN	G&T	Gifted and talented
EAL	English as an additional language	LAC	Looked after child
SS	Social services involvement	TRA	Traveller
YC	Young carer		

Individuals are complex and do not fit neatly into labels or categories, so a pupil can often be assigned to more than one 'group'. Sometimes it is also helpful to provide further detail next to the SEN levels, to provide information about what type of need the child has – for example, is it behaviour, emotional and social needs or cognition and learning?

Once this information is collated, it is easy to update and provides a simple visual reference for teachers to ensure that they fully understand the needs of the children in their cohort, and that they are using that information to plan for an appropriate teaching approach at Wave 1. Schools with which we have worked, have found it useful to update this information three times a year to coincide with the School census and to link in with the other whole school improvement processes that we discuss throughout this book.

Example Profile of Need

Child	Needs
A	**SA** Cognition and learning
B	
C	**G&T; EAL**
D	**ST** Behaviour, emotional and social difficulties
E	Behaviour, emotional and social difficulties
F	**LAC; G&T**
G	
H	**SA** Communication and interaction
I	
J	**SA** Behaviour, emotional and social difficulties
K	**SA+** Behaviour, emotional and social difficulties
L	**SA+** Cognition and learning
M	**TRA**
N	
O	**EAL**
P	**SA** Communication and interaction
Q	Behaviour, emotional and social difficulties
R	**G&T; SS**

The example above indicates a dominance in difficulties associated with behavioural, emotional and social needs – with children identified on the SEN register as having those needs, as well as other children who do not meet the criteria for placement upon the SEN register, but still at times demonstrate difficulties in the area of behavioural, emotional and social needs. This type of profile within the class will clearly impact upon the teaching style required and the levels of support, provisions and strategies required to enable the class to learn effectively.

Using the information to plan Wave 1 intervention and support appropriately ensures that the teacher does not become over-reliant upon having to put in additional intensive withdrawn Wave 2 and 3 interventions. It is important for teachers to get the balance right between withdrawn interventions and an appropriately differentiated and planned whole-class inclusive teaching approach.

By doing this simple exercise with staff, it also helps to reinforce that there is no such thing as a 'typical class' – every class or cohort will have different needs and strengths which the teacher needs to acknowledge and address. We need to move away from the class teacher who delivers the same literacy lesson at the same time of year that he or she has done for the last eight years – regardless of how the needs within each class that he or she has taught have changed each year.

Case study

Staff used an INSET day to look critically at the Waves of Intervention and how they were supporting needs across the school.

The focus for the day was planned following a realization that staff were getting overloaded and stressed by the amount of withdrawn interventions and additional support that were required to meet pupil needs.

Teachers were complaining that their lessons were continually disrupted by children leaving and entering for withdrawn intervention, and that they needed the support within their lessons. The teaching assistants felt stressed, and complained that they wasted time trying to get the children from each class to come to the planned intervention groups.

The senior leadership team decided that instead of responding by employing more support staff, they needed to critically review how support staff were being used and how pupils were being supported to make progress within their classroom environments.

During the INSET day, each teacher drew up a simple class Profile of Need. This initially took some time, as it became apparent that the teachers, although directly responsible for teaching the children, did not actually fully understand or know about the specific needs of each individual.

The learning support team, family liaison officer and members of the pastoral teams were able to provide further details to clarify when questions arose about placement upon the SEN register or social services involvement. This gave the staff an opportunity to reflect upon the importance of having first-hand knowledge about the children and how it would be impossible to fully provide a curriculum at Wave 1 which adequately meets the needs of the cohort without having this clear understanding.

Staff shared with each other the findings from the Profiles of Need, which in some cases were startling. In particular, the needs of Cohort A were considered. In this cohort every child except one had a 'need' indicated next to his or her name. Many children were placed upon the SEN register as a result of difficulties with their behaviour, and there was a dominance of boys within the cohort.

This contrasted with Cohort B, where there was a dominance of girls within the cohort, no behaviour difficulties but generally low levels of learning across all pupils – with many placed on the SEN register with cognition and learning difficulties. This cohort also contained children with EAL who had recently joined the school with little or no English.

Staff, although generally aware of the issues of some of the children in each cohort, were startled by how significant these were, and engaged in discussion and debate about how the needs of these two very different groups could be met through Wave 1. The value of using this information to aid planning for whole-class teaching was emphasized, with the teachers clearly seeing how different the approach to each class would have to be.

In Cohort A, it was agreed that Wave 1 would have to incorporate a wide range of behaviour strategies, motivational reward systems and learning styles appropriate to the mainly male-dominated cohort; whereas in Cohort B it was noted that there would need to be daily opportunities to reinforce and consolidate basic skills and concepts, and also possibilities for pre-teaching relevant topic vocabulary for the pupils with EAL.

Following from the INSET day, the staff have continued to update and use the Profiles of Need to plan whole-class teaching approaches relevant to the needs of each cohort. The Profiles of Need now take very little time to complete. Staff are skilled, informed and aware of the needs of all of the children that they teach, and the understanding achieved has impacted upon the quality of teaching and provision within the classroom at Wave 1.

As a direct result, teachers feel more equipped to differentiate and plan their lessons with the needs of the children in mind, which has in turn reduced the need for so many children to receive withdrawn intervention programmes. Support staff are used more effectively both within the classrooms and to deliver appropriate, highly structured, time-limited Wave 2 and Wave 3 interventions.

Planning additional provision should therefore build upon this carefully considered foundation of good-quality inclusive teaching which is closely matched to the need profile of the particular class cohort.

What is Wave 2 intervention?

At Wave 2, there are again a number of key issues which must be considered and addressed in order to ensure that provision at Wave 2 is effective, appropriate and efficient. Wave 2 provision is for those children who require a specific time-limited intervention or support in order for them to be able to make age-appropriate progress. One of the most important issues for schools to understand is that Wave 2 support is not for children with SEN or specific long-term needs. Indeed, in order for Wave 2 provision to be effective within a school context, it is absolutely essential that staff have clear understanding of how to identify appropriate children to access it.

Using data effectively to continually monitor the progress of all children therefore becomes key. Appropriate children to identify for Wave 2 interventions will typically be those 'middle-ability' children with no specific areas of need or difficulty who would benefit from some small-group focused support to boost or accelerate progress. Wave 2 is not intended for children with longer term needs where they will require prolonged support.

Recent terminology from the National Strategies has therefore noted that Wave 2 is not just about helping children to 'catch up'. Rather it is about ensuring that children are able to 'keep up' with their expected progress. This is significant. It means that we do not need to wait for a child to begin to fail before putting in place appropriate and effective support. Instead, we can, and should, rigorously monitor the progress of all children to be able accurately to identify immediately when a child may be in need of support to keep up with his or her potential and make expected age-appropriate progress.

Where children are accurately identified to access a Wave 2 provision, the provision is able to become focused, time-limited and specific. Staff can be clear about the exact gap or difficulty with a specific concept that needs to be addressed in more detail with an identified group of children, and can set up a provision to last for a limited amount of time, with clear outcomes, to be reviewed at a set date.

If the group have been accurately identified, once they have received the planned intervention for a specified amount of time they should be able to achieve the targeted outcomes, and then not be in need of further intervention or provision.

What is Wave 3 intervention?

Wave 3 is for more specific and individual needs, and will relate to those children who have got more significant gaps in knowledge or areas of need. It will clearly relate to those children who have specific identified individual needs and are placed on the SEN register – particularly those children who have needs identified at School Action Plus and those with statements of SEN. However, Wave 3 interventions can and should also be used to support other children across a cohort, where their needs do not fulfil the required criteria to be placed on the SEN register but who will require targeted high-level support in order to make effective progress.

It will therefore be essential for staff to refer back to their class Profile of Need to identify accurately which needs are whole-class and are therefore Wave 1 needs, and which are more individualized and will therefore require more additional support.

In some cohorts this will mean that if the level of learning across the cohort is low, and there is a need for regular reinforcement and consolidation of basic skills, then the needs of children with learning difficulties are being addressed through good-quality high-level Wave 1 provision. However, within the same cohort, there may be one or two children who are operating at a significantly higher level – perhaps four or five sub-levels above the average level of attainment of other children. These children may have been identified as being gifted and talented and they will require the highly individualized, specific Wave 3 support to enable them to move forward effectively and develop higher order thinking and learning skills.

Similarly, there may be children with English as an additional language who do not need to be identified on the SEN register, but who may require high levels of focused and additional support and provision to enable them to make progress whilst they are developing the language skills necessary to access learning in an English-speaking school context.

Whoever the Wave 3 support and intervention is planned for, it is essential that there is still a clear focus on time-limited and reviewed interventions – to help children to move away from the traditional 'resource and hope' or 'lifestyle' models of intervention and support discussed earlier.

Children who need to access Wave 3 support will need longer term support to develop key skills, but it is essential that this is broken down into appropriate small steps which can then be reviewed and monitored at regular times. Thus, it may be that a child has an identified difficulty with number concepts. The first Wave 3 provision may be to consolidate number bonds at an appropriate level in relation to their needs and, once progress towards this outcome through a structured intervention programme has been reviewed, the next small step may be introduced, again with a clear outcome and end date where progress is checked and reviewed.

This approach enables staff to have the opportunity to stop and consider whether identified methods, approaches and provisions are actually appropriate to meeting the needs of the child, and will help support staff to move away from providing inappropriate support which then is not changed or addressed until the end of a full year.

Monitoring and evaluating impact: what's working in the school?

How are interventions planned and monitored within the school context?

In addition to planning a range of appropriate provisions to support individuals and cohorts within the school, there is now a clear focus upon ensuring that the impact of that support is monitored, measured and evaluated. There is, therefore, no point in continuing to deliver a time-consuming and costly (in terms of adult resource) intervention term after term to groups of children if, on evaluation of impact in terms of measurable outcomes, there is no impact upon the children's attainment and skill levels.

This should, therefore, become an essential part of the whole process, and should be carefully considered by staff members as part of the dynamic model of Inclusion in Action that we are proposing throughout the book.

In order to support practitioners in understanding the processes involved in this stage of the model, it may be helpful to consider the following reflective questions.

Reflective questions	Reflection/comment
Do we have a clear understanding of a range of possible effective interventions that we can draw on?	
Where do we get this information from?	
How are children selected for interventions, or how are interventions selected to meet the needs of individuals or groups of children?	
How are baseline levels collated?	
How is progress monitored and measured through the intervention programme?	
How is impact at the end of the intervention programme checked and evaluated?	
How does this evaluation impact upon further strategic thinking and planning within the school setting?	

How can we gain a clear understanding about interventions which may be effective?

For a school to be able to make any reasoned, strategic decisions about which interventions to implement to address particular needs and for particular groups of children, it is essential that there is some background understanding about the intervention itself, how it works, and the potential impact or effectiveness of the intervention.

Practitioners can therefore be encouraged to seek advice from a range of available resources:

- DCSF 'What Works' guidance (www.dcsf.gov.uk/research/search/default.cfm);
- published, researched interventions, such as Reading Recovery;
- National Strategy interventions;
- localized discussions about existing good practice utilizing outside agency and professional experiences.

1. DCSF 'What Works' guidance

The DCSF (previously DfES) regularly commission in-depth research reports on the effectiveness of a wide range of intervention programmes. These include 'What works for children with literacy difficulties'; 'What works for children with numeracy difficulties'; and 'What works in developing children's emotional and social competence and well-being'. These provide some very useful information and guidance about general principles, approaches and strategies as well as specific identified intervention programmes, and practitioners can usefully use these documents to help them to develop a rationale for taking on a particular intervention within their school setting.

It is, however, also important to recognize that although there may be reported evidence of an intervention working, that does not necessarily mean that the intervention will always be successful within every setting. This will be dependent upon:

- individual school context;
- skills of key staff members and training in using the intervention programme;
- the specific area of need of the children utilizing the intervention;
- whether the intervention fits in with the wider philosophy of teaching and learning approaches within the school as a whole.

It is therefore also important to consider other ways to find out information about which interventions to develop within your school setting, and point 4 (below) is particularly significant.

Schools need to make use of published research. The following free sites have either commissioned research or are portals which enable schools to search for relevant research or provide a review of the published research in particular areas:

- DCSF Research Site: www.dcsf.gov.uk/research/
- Ofsted Publications: www.ofsted.gov.uk/Ofsted-home/Publications-and-research
- Teacher Training Resource Bank: www.ttrb.ac.uk/
- The Evidence for Policy and Practice Information and Co-ordinating Centre (EPPI-Centre): www.eppi.ioe.ac.uk/cms/
- TeacherNet: www.teachernet.gov.uk/

2   Published, marketed interventions

There are some highly used, carefully researched and documented interventions which have been developed and utilized over some time within different countries. These include interventions such as Phono-graphix and Reading Recovery.

Looking carefully at the detail, research and description of how the intervention operates will therefore give the practitioner and school staff further guidance about whether the intervention is one that could be developed for use within their particular school setting.

The benefits of such intervention programmes are that there will often have been extensive piloting and detailed research carried out and documented, which school staff will be able to utilize in their strategic decision making. There is frequently clear and convincing evidence presented about the significant or substantial outcomes achieved through the intervention programme. Indeed, the notion of the 'gold standard' of 'double the rate of progress' has come from intervention programmes such as these, where intensive, often 1:1 support is given for a prolonged, measured amount of time (e.g. 12–16 weeks) to enable significant progress to be achieved.

The limitations, however, may be that often such intervention programmes are extremely prescriptive, and this may be restrictive within the particular school setting. They may stand outside the National Curriculum or National Strategy guidance, and therefore school staff will have to find ways to ensure that their pupils are not confused by different teaching approaches.

Interventions which demand high levels of 1:1 support may also not be considered effective 'value for money' in some school settings, and this is indeed another key consideration for schools to think about.

3   National Strategy interventions

Since the introduction of the National Literacy Strategy and the National Numeracy Strategy in 1998, there has been the addition of further resources and detailed support or intervention materials developed to support children in need of further teaching and learning in particular areas of learning.

These have included the Additional Literacy Support (ALS); Further Literacy Support (FLS); Early Literacy Support (ELS); SpringBoard Numeracy; Wave 3 Mathematics; Year 3 Literacy Support – Sir Kit. In secondary schools, the Secondary Strategy has developed interventions such as Key Stage 3 Maths and English, Key Stage 4 Learning Challenge, GCSE Booster Resources.

Some of these interventions are designed for children who are middle ability, to give them a boost in developing their skills (such as the ELS); whilst others have been designed for children with significant gaps in their knowledge of a particular area (such as the Wave 3 Numeracy). It is therefore important for the practitioner to have a very clear idea about the nature and expected scope of the intervention – who it is for and how it is to be used – before implementing it within the classroom or school setting.

Schools have to consider the nature of their own particular context – and the children with whom they are hoping to utilize the intervention. Thus, whilst the interventions were originally quite prescriptive and rigid in their structure, National Strategy consultants are increasingly emphasizing flexibility of approach in utilizing the materials, strategies and teaching ideas in effective ways. Indeed, in this way, for example, the guidance within the Wave 3 Mathematics Pack not only includes suggestions for how to use the intervention to meet the specific gaps in mathematical knowledge of an identified child but also gives suggestions about how to use the resources as a Wave 2 'catch-up' or 'keep-up' resource to ensure that a small group of children keep up with the whole-class teaching content. Similarly, further useful examples are given of times where, through rigorous gap analysis, a school may have identified that a whole class has misunderstood a particular concept – and then, again, the materials and approaches are suggested for use within Wave 1 whole-class teaching.

4   *Localized discussions about existing good practice utilizing outside agency and professional experiences*

There are clearly plenty of places that the practitioner can gather information about the effectiveness of different interventions. However, the key message is about sensible reflection and questioning about the intervention in relation to the actual, individual school context.

For many schools, perhaps particularly those working with different vulnerable groups, or with children in challenging social and economic settings, it is not always easy simply to pick an intervention off a shelf and deliver it in its original form. Often, detailed thinking and planning needs to go into how the intervention could be adapted to make it effective in meeting the needs of specific children for whom it is planned within that individual context. It may, for example, only be necessary to focus on a small part of the whole intervention with a particular group, rather than the intervention in its entirety.

To support practitioners in making key strategic decisions about which interventions to use for particular needs of cohorts of children, it is therefore very useful to utilise links and partnerships both with other local schools (those working in similar situations as well as those who have developed different approaches to meet different cohort needs) and with other professionals and agencies that may be able to provide further objective advice and support based upon their experiences working with a number of different schools.

Often, the professional and reflective discussions that can be instigated between professionals working in different settings and contexts can be stimulating opportunities to enhance practitioner understanding of the issues involved in developing effective interventions, provisions and support. This is, therefore, perhaps one of the most significant points of contact for gathering information about which interventions may be useful to investigate for use within the school context, and schools should be encouraged to look at creative and innovative ways to create links and partnerships with professionals working in different settings and contexts.

How can we ensure that interventions do not take the place of good-quality Wave 1 teaching?

When scrutinizing interventions across a class, year group or school it is essential to ensure that they are not being used to replace good-quality Wave 1 teaching, or to make up for less than adequate whole-class teaching. Thus, key questions about the number of children needing to access a given intervention need to be considered. If a teacher has identified that most of the class requires further intervention support at Wave 2 and Wave 3 to address, for example, phonics or gaps in mathematical concept knowledge, then this should highlight the fact that this needs to be addressed through a change in Wave 1 teaching approach. The class may, therefore, as a whole, require daily phonics input – rather than being withdrawn in small groups, adding disruption to whole-class teaching times for withdrawn input.

Returning to reconsider what is being provided at Wave 1, and whether there are any whole-class gaps or difficulties which could effectively be addressed at Wave 1, helps to ensure that teachers and pupils do not become overloaded by too many interventions. Interventions in classes where too many withdrawn interventions have been planned to respond to needs not being adequately addressed at Wave 1 become too diluted, with not enough time or energy being able to be devoted to them for them to work effectively. The practitioner is reminded again of the pyramid model, where strategic analysis of interventions and support across the school should see more at Wave 1, with a smaller number at Wave 2 and Wave 3.

How are children identified for intervention groups?

It is essential that there is a clear system in place for identifying children in need of intervention across the class, year group or school. This should be clearly linked to an analysis of accurate and current assessment data.

Discussions should be encouraged that concern the needs of particular individuals and groups and those with more obvious long-term needs. Children who are 'coasting' or not continuing to make expected rates of progress must also be identified. Careful analysis of data is therefore central in any identification of children who require Wave 2 intervention, and where Wave 2 interventions do not work it is often because the wrong children have been selected for that intervention. Rather than identifying those children who are in need of a little bit of further support, or reinforcement of a key concept, often schools wrongly identify children who will have more prolonged intensive needs in a particular area.

For the intervention group to work, it is also important for the children to be working at a similar level and to have similar gaps in concept or skill knowledge.

There are also other considerations to be taken into account, including the social, emotional and behavioural needs of the individuals within the group, and whether they will be able to work together as a group.

When do interventions happen?

For an intervention to be effective, it needs to support rather than replace or contradict the rest of the class-based educational experience of the child. Careful consideration therefore needs to be given to when an intervention will take place. Often, interventions are planned as extra, withdrawn sessions in addition to the whole-class literacy or numeracy lesson. Whilst this model does work at times, practitioners within schools need to be very careful and mindful of the need for every child to have equal access to a broad and balanced curriculum, with full opportunities for participation.

We would recommend, therefore, that practitioners carefully consider the overall educational experience of key individuals requiring high levels of intervention and support, to ensure that their educational experience does not become too narrowly focused by a dominance and over-reliance on extra, withdrawn interventions and support in one particular area. Thus, in some schools, where staff have analysed and reflected about the day-to-day experience of key identified individuals, they have found that some children, with a particular area of need in phonics and reading and writing, spend up to 85 percent of their school week just working on this area of difficulty – both within the classroom during the whole-class teaching and also during withdrawn support groups and 1:1 support sessions. These children miss out on other areas of the curriculum where they could excel and achieve some success.

Often, class teachers can use interventions very appropriately to enhance their whole-class teaching. Thus, groups can be supported at points during the whole-class input or plenaries and can also benefit from the intervention programme as part of their group work activity within the main lesson – rather than having to do it as an extra, at a separate time.

In all, it is about creating the right balance between providing the right support for children to enable them to make progress and ensuring that they have their entitled access to a broad and balanced curriculum, where they are able to enjoy and excel in other curriculum areas.

How can interventions be planned to ensure that they are time-limited, and what are the benefits of this approach?

As previously discussed, it is essential to ensure that interventions do not become the child's 'lifestyle' – their sole educational experience. Rather, all interventions need to be carefully planned to run for a specified number of weeks – with a clear outcome set for progress made during that specified amount of time (see also discussion below). Without careful planning around a set, specified amount of time, interventions can run continuosly without rigorous monitoring.

There is no set notion of exactly how long interventions should run for – this will depend entirely upon the particular intervention selected, the type of group accessing the intervention, and whether it is a short-burst Wave 2 intervention or a more intensive, possibly more prolonged Wave 3 intervention.

How can we ensure clear, measurable outcomes for each intervention, and why is this important?

Another aspect that is often neglected in the planning and delivery of interventions, which will directly affect and impact upon the intervention's ability to be effective, is the formulation of clear measurable outcomes or objectives for the child or group of children to achieve by the end of the intervention.

All involved – teacher, staff member delivering the intervention, pupils and parents – should have a very clear idea about the objectives of the intervention, and which skills the pupil will be able to demonstrate on completion of the intervention. The effectiveness of the intervention will then be able to be evaluated and measured by analysing how many children have successfully achieved those measurable outcomes.

Practitioners will need to consider carefully where these outcomes will come from. In some curriculum areas, they may come directly from the curriculum objectives, levels of attainment, or the National Strategy Renewed Framework objectives. Practitioners may, however, find that the levels or objectives are too broad and far-reaching, and that they need to be broken down into smaller, more precise and measurable basic skills.

A focused writing intervention for a group of pupils who are still working at Level 2 in their independent writing might aim for the following measurable outcomes:

- I will be able to verbalize three full sentences independently;
- I will be able to write three full sentences independently, using
  - neat presentation;
  - correct spelling of high-frequency words;
  - phonic skills to sound out unfamiliar words;
  - full stops and question marks.

For other interventions, perhaps those which are focused upon other areas of need – for example, behavioural, social, speech and language or fine and gross motor skills – other ways to plan measureable outcomes will need to be considered. This may involve careful liaison with other outside professionals such as the speech and language therapist in the development and planning of a focused speech and language intervention.

Other interventions, including some for behavioural interventions or fine and gross motor skills, may have clear measurable outcomes built into the structure of the programme, in steps or levels, and these could be taken or adapted by the practitioner. For ease and impact, these clear measurable outcomes should be clearly identified at the start of the intervention, and shared with all involved. Progress through the intervention will then always be measured in relation to these. This means that planning demands are reduced – the intervention has already been carefully planned and new targets or outcomes will not need to be planned on a weekly basis.

Who delivers interventions?

It is important that time and consideration are given to thinking about who is actually delivering the intervention – and these reflections can also be linked with thinking about when and how the intervention is delivered. In practice, it is often teaching assistants who are directly responsible for delivering key interventions to groups of children. Where this happens, leadership teams need to think very carefully about the implications of this.

In particular, whoever delivers the intervention needs to:

- be fully aware of the needs of the children;
- understand why the particular intervention has been chosen;
- have received clear training about how to deliver the programme;
- have support to respond to the children's progress throughout the intervention.

So often, interventions are given over to teaching assistants in passing, without enough discussion, collaborative planning and training involved and, no matter how skilled the teaching assistant may be, this will always impact upon its potential to be effective.

Another key issue associated with the delivery of the intervention is the need for all staff within a school to be fully aware of the statutory duty, set out within the National Curriculum Inclusion Statement, of each teacher to ensure that he or she takes direct responsibility for the planning, teaching and learning of *every* child within the class. This is an important issue, and one that is at the heart of fully inclusive education practice. We need to ensure that all children have direct access to, and equal opportunities to participate and engage with, the qualified trained teacher within their class. School staff need to carefully review and reflect upon the day-to-day learning experience of each pupil – including those with high levels of complex learning needs. By doing this, often staff identify that some key children are actually supported to access learning activities in their classroom with qualified teachers very little – and instead, much of their educational experience is built upon withdrawn intervention support delivered by unqualified professionals within the school setting.

Overall, the important issue is to achieve a careful balance. Teaching assistants have become a highly skilled and extremely valuable resource within the education system and have a very clear role to play in supporting children who are in need of further intervention and support. However, this needs to be balanced by ensuring that *every* teacher fulfils his or her statutory duties for every pupil, by spending time working with each child, monitoring his or her progress and liaising closely with the teaching assistants to ensure that next steps are appropriately planned.

Why should progress during, at the end and after the intervention be monitored?

For interventions to be effective and to have an impact upon learning and achievement within the school setting, it is essential that clear systems are set up to monitor, review and evaluate progress throughout the intervention, and also at the end of the intervention. Linked to this, staff also need to consider ways to monitor how progress and learning through the intervention programme are transferred into whole-class learning situations.

In our experience, one of the most important issues associated with this is about ensuring that any system that is set up and developed is simple, clear, quick and easy to use. Staff often do not have either the time or inclination to complete complex recording sheets.

Staff also need to consider how the information is going to be reviewed and used. Many staff members find that they do not have time to read lengthy handwritten notes about each pupil's experience within the intervention group. Rather, a simple, visual system that records which pupils are exceeding expectation and which are underachieving is often more useful and helpful. A clear shared understanding about what needs to be recorded, and why, will therefore help staff members to develop a unique system which will work effectively for them within the context of the school – and this will then impact upon the teaching and learning experience of the individual child.

It is important for such systems to be devised in consultation with the whole staff group – and to be regularly reviewed, amended, and adapted within the school setting. This will help to achieve shared understanding and commitment towards the system set up.

Where we have seen highly effective systems in operation, the monitoring system is carefully designed around very clearly set agreed outcomes. Progress towards these outcomes can then be effectively monitored, recorded and tracked using very simple colour coding systems. Some schools have chosen to use a smiley face system to show progress: smiley face – achieved outcome; straight face – making progress towards outcome; sad face – no progress towards outcome yet. Other schools very effectively have used a traffic light system of recording progress where red demonstrates that the child is not yet making progress towards the outcome, orange indicates that the child is starting to make progress towards the outcome, and green indicates that the child has achieved the set outcome. Systems such as these can provide extremely useful ways of monitoring and tracking progress.

In addition to thinking about the systems set up to monitor progress, staff also need to consider how the information is going to be used within the school setting. In our experiences working with schools, we have seen many schools who have set up monitoring systems but who do nothing with the information gathered – which causes us to question the relevance of collating the information in the first place.

All of our work in schools has been about ensuring that such activities and systems are not just completed for the sake of it – that they are not just seen as a paper-based activity to be completed and ticked off. Instead, it is about helping all staff to understand the importance and relevance of the activity and its impact upon their daily planning for inclusive practices to support the needs of all pupils. Where this understanding is achieved, the systems that are developed become effective and meaningful.

In the case of monitoring systems, it is essential that built into discussions about developing an effective system which can be used throughout the school are also discussions and planning about how the information is going to be used, and what will happen as a result.

Where we have seen systems which work well, schools have set up clear processes for intervention monitoring records to be regularly reviewed by a range of different people at different levels throughout the school. Thus, at the first level, the person who is most responsible for delivering the intervention will use the monitoring records as a way to review on a regular basis the progress that the children are making and any areas which still need to be focused on. At the next level, this information is shared with the teacher, to ensure shared understanding, planning and reflection about the needs of the children, and how they can be supported not only during the intervention programme but also within the whole-class situation. Finally, key people in positions of leadership within the school can review the monitoring records at regular times to consider from a position of distance how the children are doing, identify any patterns or trends emerging, and think about ways to address any underlying or continuing difficulties in different ways.

At all levels, key questions need to be asked of the information given by the monitoring record:

- **Are the outcomes that have been set relevant and meaningful for the pupils?** If the pupils achieve them too early on in the intervention programme, then clearly the outcome and the intervention has been pitched at the wrong level.
- **Are the pupils starting to make progress towards the outcomes?** If there is no progress being made this may indicate that the outcomes that have been identified are too difficult and they may need to be broken down into smaller steps.

- **Are the outcomes being addressed often enough?** If too many outcomes have been identified and planned for the intervention programme, this may impact upon the ability of the children to make effective progress.
- **Are there any individuals who are not keeping up with the rate of progress of the other children?** Look carefully at possible reasons for this. One of the main reasons may be lateness or poor attendance: how many sessions has the child actually been able to attend? Or was the child wrongly identified for the intervention programme? Does he or she require something more specialized?

Rigorous monitoring of progress through the intervention enables changes to be made and the intervention overall to become more responsive to the needs of the children. There is very little point in waiting until the end of the intervention period to identify that the wrong outcomes have been set!

Monitoring sustained progress as a result of a given intervention is more difficult, but this is another key issue which needs to be considered by school staff in order to ensure that the intervention has an impact. Careful planning and monitoring need to be considered in order to ensure that opportunities are provided for pupils to transfer the skills that they have learnt into whole-class and independent learning activities.

To support the discussions already presented it may also be useful for practitioners to consider the examples of planning and recording formats given within Appendix 2.1 (see pp. 140–2).

Concluding comments

Planning for effective intervention is a key issue within schools today. School staff need to ensure a shared understanding of the range of issues associated not only with the planning and effective implementation of appropriate interventions but also with the need to reflect carefully upon good-quality Wave 1 inclusive teaching to meet the needs of all pupils.

Where school staff engage with these issues in a meaningful way, we see staff making key links between the planning of interventions and the appropriate and efficient use of a range of other systems within the school – as in the Inclusion in Action model.

By linking the processes in a meaningful way, and by ensuring that critical and reflective debate and discussion is at the heart, then self-evaluation processes will be enhanced, thinking about how to effectively develop increasingly inclusive practices will be deeper, and action in terms of prioritizing whole school developments will occur.

Practitioners can use the following reflective questions as starting points for reviewing their own practice.

Reflective questions	Reflection/comment
What has this chapter taught me about inclusive interventions?	
How does this relate to my own current practice?	
How does this relate to current strategic practice in my school?	
What are the next steps in developing more inclusive and strategic approaches to interventions in my school?	

5 Provision Mapping: The Strategic Whole School Development Tool

In this chapter we critically explore the following issues and concepts:

- What is provision mapping?
- Moving towards inclusive, whole school provision maps
- Linking provision mapping with the whole school self-evaluation and development process

Provision maps are a way of visually recording and setting out what is going on and where, within the school setting, to meet the needs of all pupils. They are crucial in supporting and enabling the development and implementation of strategic decision making to ensure that provision meets the needs of all pupils.

We see provision mapping as a central tool towards developing inclusive practices within the school setting. It is a process which clearly stands within the Inclusion in Action model, and is one of the systems that can enable the 'action' to take place. Provision mapping builds upon staff discussions about trends and patterns of underachievement, through rigorous analysis of the data (Chapter 3) and careful reflection about provision through the Waves of Intervention (Chapter 4). The system enables staff to carefully plan, record, monitor and evaluate the effectiveness of strategic decisions made about provision for all pupils. Within our model of Inclusion in Action, this process is fully inclusive – and enables the mapping and planning for provision to meet the needs of all pupils.

We liken the process of developing effective provision mapping within schools to a journey and would want individual schools to feel empowered to develop their own system for provision mapping which suits their own particular needs. The model will often be continuously evolving to respond to different circumstances and needs, and must ensure the shared commitment and ownership of the model by all staff as it develops and responds to the needs of the school community.

What is provision mapping?

Provision Mapping and Management is now being advocated by the DCSF and National Strategies (Leading on Intervention Resource – www.nationalstrategies.

standards.dcsf.gov.uk/leadingonintervention/) as an effective tool to develop school-based practices. It is a system which is being promoted for both primary and secondary schools.

Although there is this current focus within education, it must be acknowledged that there is still relatively little written to provide a critical and reflective discussion about provision maps: how they have evolved and how they are being used to support the development of inclusive processes within schools. Within the limited literature available there is, at times, interchangeable use of terms such as 'provision mapping' and 'provision management', which causes some confusion for practitioners trying to engage with the ideas. Indeed, for us, both of the terms used are problematic. Provision mapping seems to simply suggest the recording of provision, and we would argue that there is much more involved in the process than that. Conceptually there are also difficulties with associating the process that we advocate with provision management: the process is about much more than management – it is about strategic leadership and collaborative ownership – but there is no easy term to encapsulate that. We therefore use the term 'provision mapping' throughout the book for ease of understanding and use.

There have also been different emphases in terms of whether provision mapping is a tool to be used to support planning for the needs of those children with SEN, or as a more inclusive tool to plan and map provision for all pupils.

Within recent literature about provision mapping (Gross and White 2003; Gross 2008) there has been a focus upon using the tool to support vulnerable groups, particularly SEN or learners with learning difficulties and disabilities (LLDD). This has led some schools to respond to provision mapping in rather a compartmentalized way, which can lead to a narrowing of the curriculum and an increase in segregationary practice. Some schools have found it difficult to see the broader value of the tool as a means to increase participation and remove barriers for all pupils.

Provision maps have been developed to provide schools with an effective and efficient way to record the variety of interventions and provisions that are planned to respond to pupil need (Black-Hawkins *et al.* 2007). Over the years, different local authorities and schools have responded to this in different ways. In some areas, there continues to be an emphasis upon provision mapping to record the 'additional to and different from' provision or support that identified pupils with SEN receive. We believe that, although this is a useful activity, there are huge benefits to using provision mapping in a more fully inclusive way as a central part of whole school strategic decision making and planning (as demonstrated within our Inclusion in Action model).

The activity of producing provision maps should not just be seen as a paper-based, accountability exercise. Initial models that were based upon the use of provision maps to cost (in financial terms) the support that pupils were receiving reinforced this perception of them. Where effective models have developed, school staff have been involved in the process and seen their value as working documents which inform their day-to-day teaching and planning for groups of pupils.

Before moving on, it is useful for the practitioner to spend some time reflecting about how provision maps are currently used within their own school context.

Reflective questions	Reflection/comments
How are provision maps used within my school?	
Why are provision maps used?	
Who introduced them to the school context? Why?	
Who is involved in the process of provision mapping?	
Is the information recorded used on a daily basis?	
What sort of provisions and interventions are recorded on a provision map?	
What are the strengths of my current provision mapping system?	
What are the limitations?	

Moving towards inclusive, whole school provision maps

How can provision mapping be seen as more than just a paper-based activity?

Provision mapping is a central tool which can link with other school systems to enhance the planning and provision for inclusive learning experiences for all pupils. We would encourage all schools to think carefully about the benefits of such a system to support the development of inclusive whole school practices for all pupils. Our experiences have shown that, although provision mapping may seem more difficult for larger schools to engage in fully (including large amalgamated primary schools and secondary schools), where those schools do prioritize planning about how to make the system work for them there is a huge benefit in terms of full staff understanding of the complex needs of a large number of pupils, and greater awareness of the range of provision, interventions and strategies available to support all pupils.

Secondary schools wishing to develop provision mapping within their school context need to ensure that the system that they use utilizes existing practices within the school and complements current school structures. Where the school is structured and led in faculties, the most effective model of provision mapping has reflected this, by mapping provision within faculties. Some secondary schools have chosen to develop their provision mapping system to reflect vertical pastoral tutor groups, or to map provision by year group, depending upon how staff currently work within the school.

We believe that it is essential for schools to understand how to move provision mapping forward from being simply a paper-based activity or form (a stand-alone provision map) to a central tool in evaluating the school experience for all pupils. When this happens, provision maps become a strategic tool for exploring a range of different school-based issues, relating to whole school or cohort needs and how provision is planned to respond effectively to those needs. The provision map becomes not only a visual record of what is happening but, more importantly, an essential prompt to enable challenging questions to be raised about the experiences and provisions on offer. Thus the focus is not just about mapping provision onto a provision map; it is about the strategic analysis and critical reflection about the information contained within it, in order to move inclusive practices forward for all pupils.

What are the benefits of provision mapping?

There are some key benefits to developing whole school, inclusive provision mapping systems within the school context. These include the use of provision maps to provide:

- a visual and easily accessible record of provision across a school;
- an effective tool for strategic planning and management of provision;
- a unique school-based tool which can be developed by staff and for staff to ensure shared ownership and overall effectiveness.

Each of these issues is briefly discussed below.

A visual and easily accessible record of provision across a school

Provision mapping provides a visual, easy to access way to record the range of provisions, support and interventions that pupils within the school are accessing. It has traditionally been linked with the planning and mapping of provision for pupils with SEN or learners with learning difficulties and disabilities, although we promote the view that, as provision mapping is such a valuable activity, it should be extended to consider the learning experiences of all pupils within the school context.

Where a range of information is recorded relating to the educational experience of pupils across a particular cohort, the provision map provides a simple way to share that information with a number of different professionals, staff and stakeholders. SENCOs have found it helpful to use provision maps to support discussions about individual needs during multi-agency professional meetings or when requesting statutory assessment of an individual's needs. The information recorded on a provision map can also be very useful to share and communicate with parents, as it provides a broad representation of the range of support that the child may experience across a week within school. Ofsted inspectors have reported that provision maps are useful during inspections, especially now during the Renewed Inspection format where inspections are shorter, with a lighter touch. Inspectors are not able to spend so long in classrooms seeing everything that happens across the course of a day or a week. Provision maps can therefore effectively provide the information to support schools self-evaluations of the effectiveness of the systems that have been put in place.

An effective tool for strategic planning and management of provision

From the school perspective, sharing the provision maps with all staff helps all staff to understand how provision and intervention is planned and prioritized across the school. The provision maps should be used to ask challenging questions about what is currently happening, where the strengths lie, where there are gaps – and how these gaps can be filled.

In this way, provision maps become *strategic* tools for managing and planning provision – not just formats to record the provision. Where schools are engaging fully in the process the value is understood, as the provision maps become central in supporting the planning and implementation of inclusive practices and interventions for all pupils across the school. The value is transparent and visible to all within the school context.

A unique school-based tool which can be developed by staff and for staff to ensure shared ownership and overall effectiveness

It is essential for all staff members to become involved with, and engaged in the provision mapping process, and to take responsibility for recording details of the provisions and interventions available to respond to the particular needs of pupils within their class groups. This moves away from the previous model of one person (usually the SENCO) sitting down and either trying to plan and document it all herself, or trying to dash around finding out what is happening from each staff member before compiling it onto a provision map. The provision map should capture the 'reality' of the educational experience for cohorts of children. It cannot do this effectively unless the person most closely linked with planning and providing the educational experience takes responsibility for mapping the provision. By completing the activity themselves, this also offers class teachers (often working with teaching assistants and other support staff) the opportunity to review critically the needs of the pupils that they are teaching and how well their teaching style appropriately matches those needs.

What does an effective provision map look like?

There is no one way to do provision maps, and the National Strategies in their Leading on Intervention materials show a range of different models which schools have used. This is important. Schools should develop provision maps to respond to their particular school context, rather than simply filling in a given format for the sake of it.

Where schools are struggling to use provision maps effectively, it is because they are seen simply as a paper exercise, where staff are filling in a format that they do not understand. Provision mapping should be viewed as an ongoing developmental activity. It is not something that can be ticked off a 'to-do' list and neatly filed. Where schools are engaging fully with provision mapping, it links in with all other whole school processes, and staff are continuously adapting and evolving their model to respond to the other systems in place in order to make them work more effectively and efficiently together.

Schools will need to reflect carefully upon how they are going to record provision. Generally, our experiences of supporting a range of schools to develop provision mapping have shown that the most effective systems map and record provision for each class cohort. This enables in-depth analysis of the needs and provisions available for a particular cohort. This is generally seen to be more effective than mapping provision across whole year groups or key stages, as mapping in such a broad way often fails to enable close analysis of the specific and particular needs of individual class groups. Our experiences with schools often demonstrate that there are marked differences between the Profile of Needs across classes within the same year group or Key Stage, and provision mapping by each class group enables detailed reflection and strategic planning to reflect this.

There are difficulties at times with this approach, and larger primary schools and secondary schools in particular will need to consider carefully how staff are being supported to map provisions. Some of the schools that we have worked with have found it too complex to map provision by single class groups and have instead preferred to work in year groups, or across faculties. This approach has often been helpful to set up the provision mapping process initially, and to get staff informed and involved. Indeed, the process of staff working collaboratively to discuss and reflect upon the issues to record on the provision map has in some cases been a very useful advantage of working in this way. Most of the schools which have adopted this approach have found that once staff have developed understanding of the process and the issues involved, they have gradually been able to move onto setting up individual class or form group provision maps. Staff are empowered and enabled to complete the process individually and then to work collaboratively in groups to strategically review the planned provisions for pupils across a year group or key stage.

Schools should be encouraged to think carefully about the particular format for provision mapping that they wish to develop. The format should link in with existing school systems and processes and build upon existing staff knowledge. However, for the provision maps to be effective, we would suggest that they build upon the key information and column headings contained in the basic model illustrated below.

Provision	Staff/pupil ratio	Staff involved	Frequency and duration

The model presented above could be seen to be a starting point for schools, which can and should then be developed and which should evolve to suit the particular needs and characteristics of the individual school.

How can provision maps be used to inform strategic decision making within the school?

Provision maps are strategic tools and should not be used solely to record provision for groups or cohorts of children. Instead, the valuable information that has been efficiently collated needs to be used to inform strategic decision making at a whole school level.

Thus, once key information from the particular cohort or class group has been mapped onto the provision mapping format, it is essential that staff recognize that this is not the end of the activity. Rather, it should be seen as the beginning. The information recorded needs to be carefully scrutinized and analysed, with challenging questions posed about the information that is contained. This is the critical element that develops the piece of paper that outlines provision into the cyclical process of strategic overview, analysis and development of provision.

To help with this process, the box below suggests some key questions that staff members can be encouraged to ask of a completed provision map.

Checklist for completed provision map

Provision:

- Is there a range of provisions identified? If they are predominantly literacy-focused does this mean that standards in numeracy are fine, or that there is a lack of awareness within the school of appropriate interventions to raise standards in numeracy?
- Are the provisions mapped by Waves of Intervention to demonstrate the breadth and depth of learning experience within the classroom context?
- Are there provisions to meet needs other than literacy and numeracy learning needs?
- Are there provisions identified to meet the needs of all vulnerable groups – including middle-ability children who are underachieving and gifted and talented pupils?
- Have appropriate ICT strategies and interventions been identified to support the needs of particular pupils?
- Do the provisions that have been identified match the needs that have been identified through class Profiles of Need?
- Are the Literacy, Numeracy and ICT Coordinators, or heads of department, in particular involved in utilizing the information from the completed provision maps to check provision and coverage within their curriculum area?
- Is there clear age-appropriate progression within provisions – or will a pupil with difficulties with phonics be accessing the same provisions or intervention as pupils in other year groups regardless of age?
- Are the provisions appropriate? Is there consistency of approach across the school (see case study below)?

Staff/pupil ratio:

- Is the staff/pupil ratio appropriate to the intervention?
- Is the intervention likely to be successful given the particular staff/pupil ratio?
- What is the impact upon value for money, or upon an individual child's self-esteem, of having an intervention delivered 1:1?
- How could pupils be supported through small-group support?
- What is the impact of delivering an intervention to too big a group of children?
- Is any one child or group missing too much whole-class teaching?

Staff involved:

- Is the intervention or support always being delivered by a teaching assistant?

- What is the impact of this upon the quality of the intervention; upon the ability of the child to transfer the skills into a whole-class teaching and learning situation; and upon the teaching assistant, who may feel overloaded?
- What is the impact upon vulnerable or needy pupils with learning difficulties or special educational needs, if they rarely have access to the qualified professional (the teacher) within the classroom context?
- Does the pupil, or particular group, feel part of the whole-class or are they always sent out with the teaching assistant to complete differentiated intervention programmes?
- How are they supported to make progress, access whole-class teaching and be part of the wider class group?
- How is the teacher meeting his or her statutory duties as set out in the National Curriculum Inclusion Statement (DES 1999), which states that it is the teacher's responsibility to set appropriate learning challenges to meet the needs of every child within the class and to monitor progress rigorously? Is there training for all teachers in areas of SEN so they all feel confident in strategies and differentiation for all areas of need in their class – quality first teaching.
- Has the member of staff involved had adequate training to deliver the intervention or support?
- Does the member of staff involved have opportunities to liaise with other professionals to discuss, monitor and review progress that is being made through the intervention programme?

Frequency and duration of the intervention:

- Is the intervention delivered regularly enough for it to be effective and for pupils to be able to make progress as a result of it?
- Is the intervention time-limited – i.e. is there a clear indication of how long it will run for, and when impact and progress will be measured?

Case study 1

Staff worked together during a staff INSET day to share provision maps that had been completed by teachers in order to start to discuss and evaluate critically the effectiveness of the interventions that had been planned, and to identify any gaps in provision.

During the discussions it was noted that there was an inconsistent approach to supporting pupils with difficulties with phonics across the school. As a result of this, some pupils were receiving support using four or five completely different and conflicting phonics approaches.

Staff realized that although they had recently had a staff meeting to agree a consistent whole school approach to the teaching and support of phonics difficulties, this had not been effectively implemented. It was noted that, despite a whole school approach to the teaching of phonics being identified on the School Development Plan and regular monitoring of phonics by the Literacy Coordinator, or head of the English department, still this had not been noticed.

The process of coordinators taking time to scrutinize the completed provision maps was affirmed as a valuable and efficient way to ensure consistency of approach across the school.

Case study 2

The SENCO within a very large school had attended training about provision mapping, after which she wanted to consider ways to adapt the process to support the transfer of knowledge and understanding about the needs of pupils with SEN, and planned interventions and support to meet those needs.

In discussions with members of the senior leadership team, it was agreed to trial a system which would be centred around the pastoral support team, who worked most closely with children on the SEN register. All members of staff involved in the pastoral support team worked together to identify key provisions and support currently available for pupils within each year group.

This activity helped to identify some provisions which were being delivered 1:1 but which would actually benefit a small group of children. Adaptations to the existing manner of providing support were therefore made during the development of the initial provision maps.

Once the initial provision maps had been developed, they were shared with all teachers and the SENCO presented them formally to the senior leadership team. Feedback about the effectiveness of the system was collected from all staff members after three months to inform the further development of the provision maps.

Most members of staff indicated that there were clear benefits of the approach – that, as teachers, they felt much more informed about the nature of strategies and interventions available to support pupils with complex needs. They commented that they were able to use the information to focus their planning and the support available during their own lessons.

Staff members also suggested that they would like the information to be further extended and developed in order to record provisions and interventions available for those middle-ability children needing 'booster support' – and also for gifted and talented pupils.

This development was agreed by the senior leadership team and it was also agreed that, to be able to ensure full staff ownership, understanding and involvement with the developing school system, provision mapping would be identified as a key whole school priority on the annual School Development Plan. This enabled regular time to be set aside during a range of staff INSET opportunities – including whole-staff INSET as well as faculty and year group INSET activities.

The senior leadership team agreed that only by making it a high whole-school priority would the process be discussed and valued by all. It was seen to be essential that all members of staff would be involved – and it was recognized that a considerable amount of time would need to be devoted to ensuring that the developing system was meaningful and effective.

Over the year, a number of revisions and adaptations to the system needed to be made – and this was done through discussion and with the agreement of all members of staff. Staff at the school admit that it was a difficult process to go through at times but that, looking back, the focus enabled by making it a whole school development plan priority ensured the development of a fully effective and meaningful system which had the full commitment of all staff. Staff also reflected that the process of discussing pupil needs and interventions itself prompted further professional dialogue and a raising of professional discourse within the school.

Individual schools should be encouraged to think carefully about how to set up systems to encourage the linking of reflective thinking with clear strategic planning and action.

Schools which have developed an effective approach to ensure that the provision maps become part of strategic review and planning have utilized a number of different approaches to ensuring that staff members at all levels are involved in evaluation and review of the provision maps.

These have included the use of:

- regular, planned whole-staff meeting times to share different provision maps and to identify strengths and gaps in provisions;
- times to review in detail the use of age-appropriate provisions within key stage or faculty meetings;
- regular, planned senior leadership team meetings to review all of the provision maps strategically and to identify resource, training and future whole school priority issues from them.

How can provision maps be developed to reflect the particular school context effectively?

Once schools have built systems to engage fully with a range of critical and challenging questions, they should be encouraged to develop their provision mapping format further to suit the individual context and situation of their particular school. This should reflect and link in with other whole school systems and processes and how these are used, and should also reflect staff characteristics and how members of staff work together. It should be an evolving process which fully engages everyone within the school context and for which individual staff members can take ownership and fully understand the value of the activity.

Schools which have been developing the provision mapping process over some years have found it useful to add in other information to the key information outlined above, including (although this list is neither prescriptive nor exhaustive):

- mapping by Wave of Intervention;
- entry and exit data;
- type of group – to indicate which particular need type the intervention relates to. For example, is it a provision for gifted and talented pupils/pupils with EAL/pupils with SEN?
- how is progress going to be measured?
- baseline skill level and expected age-appropriate skill level.

At this point, it may be helpful to consider the example provision mapping formats included within Appendices 3.1 and 3.2 – although care needs to be taken to ensure that the format developed within the particular school accurately reflects the context of the individual school (see pp. 148–9).

It must be noted, however, that if there is an attempt to capture too much information onto the provision map too quickly, without the full understanding and commitment of all staff, then the provision maps again lose their value. Each additional piece of information that is added must be added for a reason; if and when a piece of information becomes less than useful, it can be taken off the recording form.

Case study

The SENCO had attended training about provision mapping and could see the value that it held for developing inclusive processes within her school setting. She introduced the basic provision map (outlined above) at staff meeting times, and worked with staff members to compile initial provision maps. These were introduced at staff meeting so that all staff could work together to see the value of them as strategic planning tools.

After using the same format for 18 months, members of staff within the school setting suggested adding an additional column to reflect the 'type of group' that the provision was planned for. Class teachers commented that this helped to focus their thinking when compiling their provision map and ensured that they thought not just about the SEN pupils but also about other vulnerable groups – particularly gifted and talented pupils and pupils with English as an additional language. At the same time, the school staff agreed to start to map their provisions through the Waves of Intervention. For some time, staff had been talking and reflecting about good-quality Wave 1 teaching, and it seemed important to reflect this within the provision maps that were being produced.

Four months later, the Assessment coordinator, during a senior leadership team meeting, suggested that it may be useful to include a column about how progress would be measured – to enable staff to think about ensuring that progress through interventions was tracked and monitored. Staff agreed with the addition, and added full details about different ways that progress through particular interventions could be recorded.

Some time later, at a whole-staff INSET day, class teachers and teaching assistants discussed together whether it would be useful also to include general information about baseline and exit level data, so that all staff involved in the intervention could clearly see who the intervention was aimed at and expected rates of progress. This was agreed with all staff and added to the school provision mapping format, resulting in the format below.

Provision	Type of group	Staff/ pupil ratio	Staff involved/ cost in time	Entry level data	Exit level data	How progress will be measured

This format was used successfully within the school for over a year, whilst other systems evolved and were adapted to respond to the developing whole-school systems through the school. During this time, other formats for rigorously planning focused interventions were developed within the school.

During a whole-staff review of provision maps, staff noticed that some of the information that used to be so relevant and useful was now not being completed so fully, and in fact staff were filling in some columns (particularly the entry and exit data and the column about how progress will be measured) simply because they had to, rather than with any degree of reflection or purpose. The information that had been previously held in this column was now effectively and more fully recorded on other school-based formats. This was discussed and it was agreed that the staff wanted to keep the provision maps purposeful and useful and that to include any columns where staff were not fully engaged with the information would be to reduce the usefulness and value of the provision map as a whole.

Provision maps then moved back to the previous version:

Provision	Staff/pupil ratio	Staff involved	Frequency and duration	Type of group

Linking provision mapping with the whole school self-evaluation and development process

Why is it important for provision mapping to link with other systems and processes?

Throughout this book, we emphasize the value of moving towards viewing systems and processes in a more inclusive and strategic way. The Inclusion in Action model therefore suggests that each system should not be viewed as a discrete and individual activity to complete, but that rather it should be seen as an integral part of a whole school development process. We also suggest that effective systems, including provision mapping, should not just be linked to mapping provision for one vulnerable group; rather, these effective and efficient systems should be extended to support whole school strategic reflection and discussion about how the needs of all pupils are supported and prioritized.

In order for schools to be able to move forward it is essential that there is whole-staff ownership of the system and, linked to this, clear understanding of the value of the system. Individual staff members must understand why they are completing provision maps and the value that the completed provision maps have in enhancing everyday teaching and learning opportunities.

For us, it is essential that schools understand how provision mapping links as an integral component of a whole school strategic model of development. Provision mapping should not be seen as a stand-alone, or one-off process which is separate to everything else that is happening within the school to support the tracking of pupils' progress and the identification of effective and appropriate provision to meet all needs and to raise attainment and achievement for all.

Schools therefore need to consider carefully the current systems and processes employed within the particular setting and reflect upon how these currently work together to support staff understanding and planning for need, and also how the systems can be further developed.

How can pupil progress review meetings support the development of a dynamic and interlinked approach to whole school processes?

Many schools are now moving forward to utilize provision mapping as a key process within regular pupil progress review meetings. By doing this, the provision map becomes live and vibrant – a working document which is informed by and which informs all planning for the provision for all pupils. The provision mapping system is therefore in process with strategic overview of provision, which is informed by analysis of tracking, collaborative decision making and self-evaluation.

Pupil progress review meetings have recently been recommended by the National Strategies (DCSF 2007d). We see these being a very powerful tool in enabling the development of meaningful professional dialogues and critical reflection about the particular needs of specific cohorts, groups and individuals within a school setting. We consider that they can become the forum for innovative, positive, collaborative, problem-solving, supportive discussions. This is then the place where careful thinking and reflection about needs is translated into practical planning for real action. This is indeed the essence of the Inclusion in Action model that we propose – the linking of detailed reflection (self-evaluation) with careful strategic and inclusive planning (inclusion), leading to concrete action (school development) to impact upon the learning experience of the pupil.

Schools are encouraged to evolve the pupil progress review meetings to suit the particular needs and context of their own school setting (DCSF 2007d), and this is certainly a principle that we would advocate.

However, there are some key guiding principles which would support practitioners in ensuring that the meetings become as meaningful and effective as possible. The National Strategies (DCSF 2007d) provides a useful document entitled *Pupil Progress Meetings: Prompts and Guidance*, which practitioners may also wish to refer to, but the principles outlined below relate to our experiences in supporting schools engaging in this process in an inclusive and meaningful way.

Purpose:

- To provide **time** for a planned discussion about pupil progress at regular intervals through the school year.
- To emphasize the **value** of professional dialogue and reflection in supporting more effective planning to meet the needs of **all** pupils.
- To provide a **collaborative** and **problem-solving** arena for sharing discussions both about areas that have gone well and areas that need further improvement.
- To emphasize **shared responsibility** for ensuring pupil progress – underachievement is not just the responsibility of the individual teacher.
- To provide a **supportive environment** for planning future action and strategies or support that needs to be developed to accelerate pupil progress in specific areas.
- To bring together key members of staff who together can share their **different perspectives** on how to make innovative changes to practice at Waves 1, 2 and 3 to enhance pupil progress.
- To provide an opportunity to **reflect critically** upon data analysis and intervention planning in relation to effective pupil progress.

Process:

- Agree which key members of staff will attend the meeting. This will depend upon the school itself but may include: members of the leadership team (to enable strategic thinking and planning); the SENCO or interventions leader; the teacher and any support teachers or assistants working closely with the class; the receiving teacher (if the meeting is happening at the end of an academic year).
- Plan release time during the school day to enable value to be placed upon the process and to demonstrate shared commitment towards the process.
- Ensure that all members of staff attending the meeting have copies of assessment tracking data, provision maps and class Profiles of Need.
- Start the discussions with a brief opportunity for the teacher to review what has worked well for the class, groups or individuals; use the information to inform strategic planning for support and provision across the school.

- Look at any areas of underachievement. Talk supportively about what has not worked so well, and the implications of this for future Waves 1, 2 and 3 teaching and provision.
- Review the class Profile of Need and look at any trends or patterns in achievement or underachievement within particular vulnerable groups. Discuss possible strategies and interventions which may be used or adapted to meet those needs.
- Identify key training needs in relation to supporting the teacher or any support staff to understand and meet specific needs more fully within the class group.
- Strategically review current allocation of resources for the class group, including the allocation of teaching assistant support: is it effective, or do changes need to be made?

In schools which have used this system fully, all staff involved have found the experience to be extremely valuable. The meeting becomes an innovative and exciting opportunity for shared discussion and problem solving, and supports the teacher to realize that he or she is not alone in having to respond to the individual needs of his or her class because there is shared responsibility across the school. Discussions can, and should, become reflective, innovative and creative; different perspectives are shared to create new thinking and new ways to consider 'old' problems of underachievement.

We have found that an extremely valuable way to capture the dynamic and innovative problem-solving discussions is to have one person record the discussions onto a provision mapping format during the meeting.

This has a number of benefits:

- It enables the variety of new ideas to be captured and retained.
- It is a good use of time as it releases the teacher from having to write the provision map at a different time, but also ensures that the teacher has full ownership of the ideas.
- It enables a very detailed provision map to be completed before the beginning of a new term, which can then be used as a working document to plan for and provide further support and intervention immediately – rather than having to wait for information to be gathered and for the class teacher to write the provision map.

Practitioners may find it helpful to review the example provision mapping formats linked to pupil progress review meetings contained within Appendices 3.3 to 3.5 (pp. 150–3).

Concluding comments

Provision maps have evolved over a number of years and are now strongly recommended as an efficient way to map and record provisions within a school context. We believe that the use of them can be more fully explored to emphasize the value of using the simple format as a way to enable more strategic thinking and planning for inclusive practices to meet the needs of all pupils. For us, provision maps are a central tool and process within the Inclusion in Action model, which links critical questioning and reflection about current practice (self-evaluation) with the planning and implementation of practical solutions and provisions to meet a range of needs more inclusively (inclusion and school development).

Recent developments within education have seen the emergence of approaches such as pupil progress review meetings and we see this as extremely positive. We would urge practitioners and school leaders to make full use of such systems but to ensure that the key principles and values which enable them to become so effective are retained. It would be very easy for the meetings to become rather negative and punitive if the focus is on pupil deficits. The key principles that need to be emphasized would therefore include the need for the meetings to be:

- valued by all;
- supportive;
- strategic;
- reflective;
- enabling;
- collaborative;
- problem-solving;
- innovative;
- creative.

Practitioners can use the following reflective questions as starting points for reviewing their own practice.

Reflective questions	Reflection/comment
What has this chapter taught me about inclusive provision mapping?	
How does this relate to my own current practice?	
How does this relate to current strategic practice in my school?	
What are the next steps in developing more inclusive provision mapping in my school?	

6 Effective target setting for all pupils

In this chapter we critically explore the following issues and concepts:
- Developing learning for all through a personalized curriculum
- Clarifying SEN target setting
- Child-centred target setting
- Assessment for learning

Target setting is an extremely powerful tool within the school system. It enables the strategic discussions and planning raised through data analysis and provision mapping to be translated into daily practice. We believe that where targets are meaningful and inclusive they can support teachers, pupils and parents to work together to improve outcomes for all pupils and to accelerate pupil progress. Where they are not used well they become simply another administrative task within the school cycle: a paper-based activity which has little impact and influence upon the day-to-day learning experience of the individual pupil.

Target setting is another example of a central, school-based process, which is often viewed as a discrete activity and sits apart from other processes within the school. Historically, schools have focused on using target setting to meet their statutory duties with regard to the needs of children identified with SEN and placed upon the SEN register. Now, many schools are also effectively embedding curricular targets for all pupils into class-based teaching in order to make the process of setting challenging numerical targets for pupil progress at school level more meaningful and achievable to teachers and pupils (DfES 2006c). Target setting should not be seen as a separate activity within the school, and this chapter demonstrates how target setting interrelates with all of the previously discussed whole school approaches within the Inclusion in Action model. In this way, targets will become meaningful and pupils and teachers will be supported in enabling all to achieve.

Developing learning for all through a personalized curriculum

To become more inclusive, we argue that schools must aim to develop a curriculum which engages and supports the learning and enjoyment of all students. This is reflected in the language of key governmental policy and reforms such as the Every

Child Matters agenda and also the move towards personalized learning. This is a term that is now in widespread use as a result of a number of DCSF initiatives, including the new *2020 Vision* document (DfES 2006a). However, it is important to reflect carefully upon what this actually means in practice, as it is easy for schools to use the term without clear understanding of what this means in practice and how it can impact upon pupil progress. According to *2020 Vision*:

> ### *Personalizing learning is ...*
> ### *... learner-centred and knowledge-centred ...*
>
> Close attention is paid to learners' knowledge, skills, understanding and attitudes. Learning is connected to what they already know (including from outside the classroom). Teaching enthuses pupils and engages their interest in learning: it identifies, explores and corrects misconceptions. Learners are active and curious: they create their own hypotheses, ask their own questions, coach one another, set goals for themselves, monitor their progress and experiment with ideas for taking risks, knowing that mistakes and 'being stuck' are part of learning. Work is sufficiently varied and challenging to maintain their engagement but not so difficult as to discourage them. This engagement allows learners of all abilities to succeed, and it avoids the disaffection and attention-seeking that give rise to problems with behaviour.
>
> ### *... and assessment-centred*
>
> Assessment is both formative and summative and supports learning: learners monitor their progress and, with their teachers, identify their next steps. Techniques such as open questioning, sharing learning objectives and success criteria, and focused marking have a powerful effect on the extent to which learners are enabled to take an active role in their learning. Sufficient time is always given for learners' reflection. Whether individually or in pairs, they review what they have learnt and how they have learnt it. Their evaluations contribute to their understanding. They know their levels of achievement and make progress towards their goals.
>
> (DES 2006a)

We would support this view of learning in the sense that it appears to put the pupil at the centre of the learning experience. It demands that teachers and schools review their practice and settings in the light of an increasing understanding of the impact they have on enabling learning to take place. If schools are able to view the personalized learning agenda as an opportunity to support the development of more inclusive practices in school through a reflective review of existing pedagogies then there should be a positive impact on outcomes for all students. It remains to be seen whether this holistic vision of learning is reflected in the way that school effectiveness will be measured by the current and future governments.

It is important to have an opportunity to consider how target-setting practices are currently used within your own school context. Spend some time considering the reflective questions below, before moving on.

Reflective questions	Reflection/comments
Are targets set for all pupils for maths, reading, writing and science within my school?	
Is there a relationship between class-based targets / subject targets and SEN targets? How is this achieved?	
Who sets the targets, and how are they shared with pupils and parents?	
How do the targets inform daily teaching and planning activities?	
How is information about targets shared with other key staff members involved in teaching or working with the pupil?	
How are targets reviewed and how does the review inform future strategic planning?	
How do current target setting systems fit in with the notion of 'personalized learning' presented above?	

Clarifying SEN target setting

What are the statutory duties in relation to the writing of Individual Education Plans (IEPs) and targets for pupils with SEN?

The setting of meaningful targets for pupils with SEN is a statutory duty set out within the SEN Code of Practice (DfES 2001). However, confusion has abounded about the need to complete separate Individual Education Plans (IEPs) for all pupils placed on the SEN register. Although the SEN Code of Practice clearly states that targets must be set and reviewed for children identified on the SEN register, and that pupils and parents must be involved in the process of target setting, the Code of Practice does not actually stipulate that this has to happen on an IEP. Many practitioners have become confused by this notion, believing that it has been the IEP rather than the key principles (e.g. meaningful target setting and review of progress towards the target, and involvement of pupils and parents in the target setting) which has been mandatory.

As a direct result of this confusion, many schools have continued a confusing and meaningless system of writing SEN IEPs without question for all pupils identified on the SEN register. These schools follow the process of completing the paperwork without clear understanding of the key principles and values which we would suggest lie behind the setting of targets and which make the process meaningful and have impact for both teacher and pupil.

We would not wish to suggest that IEPs should be banished out of hand. Indeed, for some pupils and for some school contexts they are absolutely essential and are very valuable and meaningful systems to support the planning for accelerated progress. There are also key times and situations when IEPs are key documents, including during Annual Reviews for pupils with a Statement of SEN; when proceeding with Statutory Assessment of a pupil's needs; and when a pupil's needs are specific and are additional to and different from aspects generally covered within day-to-day classroom teaching. This will often be when the child has problems not just associated with learning needs – specific speech and language or physical needs, for example.

What is needed to ensure that IEPs and target setting are meaningful is a full understanding of the key principles behind the writing of targets for pupils with SEN and an understanding, and careful practical planning, of how those targets can then impact upon the pupil's day-to-day learning experience.

Before moving on to reflect upon some of key issues relating to meaningful target setting, consider the case study presented below.

- How meaningful are the targets being set?
- What does it tell us about the value given to target setting within the school context?

Case study

IEPs have been used within the school context to meet the needs of pupils identified on the SEN register for some years. Despite the cohort of pupils changing during this time, with an overall increase in the numbers of pupils identified on the SEN register, there has been no whole school or strategic review of the target-setting process.

Targets are set for each child placed on the SEN register three times a year.

The SENCO writes the targets for each child, and these are based upon information that she has stored about their primary need, given to her by the teachers when the child is first identified and placed on the SEN register.

The target-writing process takes some time. The SENCO does not enjoy ICT and finds it difficult and time-consuming to input all of the information onto the target format each time.

The SENCO gives the completed target forms to the teachers to file in their SEN files. Sometimes, this does not happen until quite some time into the term, as it has taken the SENCO so long to type up the information, and other priorities get in the way.

All children placed on the SEN register are given a period of allocated time during the week when they are withdrawn from the classroom and work either 1:1 or in a small group with a teaching assistant on their IEP targets. At the end of the target period, the SENCO talks to the teaching assistant who has supported the 1:1 or small-group target time to see which children have made progress with their targets.

If any child has not achieved his or her target, then the target is repeated for the next term.

The SENCO is not too disappointed if children have to repeat their targets, as this reduces the amount of time-consuming paper work that she has to complete.

A number of key issues and principles for setting targets can be identified from the case study presented above. Consider each question in relation to your own school context and current practice, before reading further for a brief critical discussion of each issue.

Reflective questions	Reflection/comments
How often are targets set within my school context? Is this an effective time span?	

Who sets the targets? How is this achieved?	
How has the target-setting process been decided upon? Has there been a whole school strategic review and evaluation of current target-setting procedures? Have changes been made? Do changes need to be made to current systems and processes?	
How are targets integrated into day-to-day classroom teaching practices?	
How are pupils supported to make progress with their targets? Do they know what their targets are? Do they know how they can achieve them?	
How is progress at the end of the target period reviewed and monitored? What happens if a child has not achieved his or her target?	

How often should targets be set?

There is no set amount of time for how often targets have to be set. However, as with the discussions presented earlier about how often to assess pupil progress, a reason-able amount of time needs to be given to enable pupils to make effective progress and to achieve their target. Generally, targets are set three times a year within schools; this amount of time enables the targets that are set to be meaningful and challenging and gives time for the child to achieve the target.

Whilst this often does work, it is important for practitioners to set up clear systems for reviewing and monitoring progress towards the target throughout the target period.

Practitioners should work responsively to the pupil's needs so where a child achieves the target set in a shorter amount of time, it is important to have a system that allows the target to be extended, or further targets added to enable further progress by the child, rather than wasting time working on a target that the child can already complete.

Who should be involved in target-setting procedures?

For the targets to be meaningful, teachers must be fully involved in the process. Often, for targets relating to pupils with SEN, the SENCO may also be involved in an advisory capacity. However, it is essential that most of the thinking and planning towards the target comes directly from the teacher.

It is often helpful for this to evolve through professional dialogue and reflection with other key people within the school (including the SENCO and school leaders). This can effectively be achieved through the pupil progress review meetings (see Chapter 5).

When SENCOs develop the targets alone, although the targets may be very carefully planned, utilizing the SENCO's specialist knowledge and expertise, they are often unable to be transferred effectively into the classroom context by the teacher.

It is essential that the teacher has ownership of the targets: that he or she fully understands the needs of the individual pupil and how to break down those areas of difficulty into managing and stretching targets – and that he or she is able to relate that to his or her day-to-day planning for the whole class.

In addition to clear involvement and ownership by the teacher, it is a statutory duty that parents and pupils should be meaningfully involved in discussions and decision making regarding the setting of targets. This will obviously happen in different ways, according to the age of the pupil and other existing school-based systems for involving parents.

Is the target-setting process still relevant and meaningful?

It is interesting for school staff to reflect upon this question. Very often, in our experiences, the target-setting process in operation within the school for children with SEN has remained the same over many years and there has been little critical review of the practice.

It is often valuable to provide time for staff to review critically and evaluate the effectiveness and meaningfulness of current systems, in order to ensure that there is still value within the activity and that is has not become so familiar that it is just seen as another paper-based activity to be completed at certain times in the school calendar. In one school in which we have worked, we observed that the system had become so over-familiar that the SENCO and class teachers were actually taking targets that had previously been set for other children – along with the related strategies and support – and cutting and pasting them directly onto new IEP formats for different children – regardless of whether the child's individual needs actually matched at all!

A critical question that needs to be considered at this stage by all practitioners is how the existing target-setting systems relate to and link in with the other school-based processes and systems to support pupil progress; this will be considered further in the next section of this chapter. Often practitioners find contradictory and competing systems at work within the school context and it is therefore essential for all practitioners to have a clear understanding of a process that works for all pupils.

How are targets integrated into day-to-day practice? How are pupils supported to make progress?

These are key questions to ask of the effectiveness of existing target-setting systems within the school context.

For pupils to be able to make meaningful progress in relation to their needs, the targets that are set must be appropriate to their needs and must be utilized fully in the planning for day-to-day learning experiences within the classroom context.

Both class teacher and individual pupil must be fully aware of the pupil's particular targets and of the small steps needed for that pupil to be able to make progress towards the target. Parents should also be involved within this process and must have a clear understanding of their child's targets and the strategies and support in place for their child to be able to achieve them.

Key questions need to be raised about how effective systems are developed to enable pupils, staff members and parents to review on a regular basis progress towards each target and to identify any remaining areas of difficulty. Day-to-day learning experiences within the classroom should be planned to ensure that the pupil is given opportunities to transfer developing skills into different contexts, and marking and feedback systems should also appropriately reinforce progress towards targets.

How is progress at the end of the target period reviewed?

For target setting to have an impact upon pupil progress, it is essential that effective systems are set up to enable pupils, parents, teachers and others to review the progress that has been made during the target period (see example in Appendices, 2.1–2.4 pp. 140–6).

Clear systems for monitoring regular progress during the target period should be set up to enable ongoing review and evaluation of the effectiveness of the targets for individual pupils. Built into these systems should be opportunities for discussion with the pupil about progress that has been made and any remaining areas of difficulty.

Simple pupil-friendly systems for recording this information can be developed, which utilize visual symbols to represent progress towards a given target. This could include smiley face symbols or a traffic light recording system.

Where a pupil has not achieved the target at the end of the target period, this would indicate the need for deeper consideration and reflection about the pupil's underlying area of difficulty and possible reasons why he or she had not made adequate progress in a particular area. Practitioners should be advised not simply to repeat the same target again. Instead, detailed reflection about the underlying causes of lack of progress will help to structure further planning in relation to developing a more effective target.

There can be a number of possible reasons for a pupil not fully achieving a given target, some of which are outlined below.

- The target was too broad, so did not allow the child to achieve it fully: next time the target should be more specific to enable progress.
- The target was too specific, and concentrated on an area which was not supported within day-to-day learning experiences: next time the target (even speaking and listening or behaviour targets) should be linked into realistic, everyday, class-based tasks and learning activities to enable the child to make progress.
- The pupil has had a lot of absences so has missed opportunities to make progress with the identified target: next time the target will need to be further broken down, and more work will need to be done with home on encouraging attendance at school.
- The support in place to enable the child to make progress with the target did not happen: next time the target will need to relate to strategies and support that will be utilized within the classroom situation. Staff within the school will need to monitor strategically and check that support, when planned, is happening.
- The target was not appropriate to the child's particular learning style: e.g. some children have considerable difficulties developing adequate phonological awareness skills. For some (including some pupils with Downs Syndrome) it becomes more appropriate to utilize whole-word strategies than continuing to work on a skill which is almost impossible for the child to master: next time the target will need to build upon the child's specific learning needs and learning style.

How can we ensure a link between SEN targets and meaningful class-based targets?

All children should now have targets set regularly for reading, writing, maths and science. There is therefore a need for whole school staff to review systems in place for setting and supporting these targets and how this fits in with SEN target (IEP) systems.

A key theme throughout the book is the need for whole-staff groups to develop shared understanding of, commitment to, and responsibility towards key systems and processes in order for them to become more effective, inclusive practices.

All staff members therefore need to have the opportunity to reflect upon the value and use of target setting within their school context, and how pupils are supported to achieve their targets effectively.

Over the last few years, a number of different systems for developing class-based targets for all pupils have emerged, including the introduction, through the National Strategies of a notion of whole school layered targets (DfES 2006b). Whilst there are some benefits of such approaches, we have seen that there is a danger of school staff blindly following systems which do not actually work in supporting progress for all pupils within their school context. In some cases, staff have lost sight of the underlying key principles of setting meaningful, personalized targets, through following a whole school system.

There are clear benefits for some schools in developing whole school layered curricular targets. In particular it:

- supports the strategic analysis of patterns of underachievement and some professional discussion and reflection about underlying causes for this underachievement;
- supports the careful planning and breaking down of specific areas of the curriculum into stages of progression;
- supports the development of professional knowledge about skill level in relation to specific areas of the curriculum at different stages through the school;
- ensures a whole school focus on a specific area of underachievement or difficulty within a curriculum area;
- encourages whole-staff discussion and further careful reflection about the learning and teaching needs required for pupils to make progress in that specific area;
- encourages and provides opportunities for staff to observe each other and to share examples of good practice to enhance the teaching and planning for specific areas of the curriculum with other staff.

However, despite these advantages, we believe that schools continue to need to reflect upon whether set whole school targets actually meet the specific needs of individual pupils. Consider the case study and the reflective questions below.

Case study

Literacy and Numeracy Coordinators within a school with a wide range of ability, with a relatively high proportion of children placed upon the SEN register, had recently attended some training about layered curricular targets.

They were enthusiastic about the system and could see benefits for reducing paperwork and the amount of time it currently took to plan effective learning targets for each child.

Information about the new systems was initially shared with the leadership team, where a strategic decision was made to adopt the system across the whole school.

Members of the leadership team acknowledged the importance of all staff sharing ownership of the new system and of fully understanding the benefits of such an approach, so time was prioritized during a whole-staff INSET day and an outside professional was invited to speak to the staff.

Staff were initially enthusiastic with the change in system. They could clearly see that it would reduce time and paperwork for them as individual teachers, and could see the benefits in enabling further whole school understanding and focus on key areas of underachievement.

A specific area of underachievement was identified and a whole school layered target system was implemented to target appropriate use of different writing formats to structure writing.

The system was developed and implemented within the school, utilizing the Must, Should and Could system of allocating specific targets to pupils in each year group. All pupils were expected to achieve the age-related 'should' target; those with SEN 'must' achieve a target just below age-related, and those who were more able 'could' achieve a target just above age-related.

Staff agreed that the system had reduced paperwork and had enabled a more detailed analysis and focus upon key areas of underachievement within curriculum areas. However, after some time, staff identified that the system was not working for many of their pupils.

Many of the pupils with SEN were operating significantly below age-appropriate levels. Writing targets, even at the 'must' (just below age-related) level were much too difficult for the pupils to achieve. Where previously staff had thought that this might help to accelerate progress for those pupils, in fact the target was so far above their current skill level that progress was not accelerated and teaching of skills related to their actual level of functioning was ignored. By targeting the 'must' area, focus was taken away from the actual skills that developmentally the child needed to work on. Thus, children who could not yet verbalize, construct and write a simple sentence were expected to achieve targets relating to the appropriate use of paragraphs to structure writing.

As children failed to achieve their targets, so the target was repeated. Pupils became uninterested and demotivated by their targets, knowing that they could not achieve them, and parents lost motivation to support them at home.

Reflective questions	Reflections/comments
Do whole school layered curricular targets support personalized learning?	
How is the whole school layered curricular target identified?	
Will this meet the learning needs of all pupils?	
How can other areas of need be effectively targeted?	

It is also interesting to consider how the use of whole school layered curricular targets fits with the notion of meaningful pupil progress review meetings (discussed in Chapter 5). The focus there was upon discussion of class, group and individual specific needs ensuring accurate and responsive planning to meet the needs identified through in-depth analysis and reflection about the actual needs of the cohort.

When a target-setting system has been identified at a whole school level and in isolation – without the depth of thinking about class, group and individual specific factors and patterns of need – how can it respond to the actual needs of individual pupils and cohorts and raise pupil outcomes effectively? Whilst the whole school layered curricular target may relate to an area of general underachievement, it is not often the basic and primary area of need for every child. Often more basic and central learning skills and concepts can be missed by focusing on the development of targets in such a way. In our experience, we have found that in schools where there is a very wide range of ability within classes, where pupils are operating significantly below age-appropriate levels with significant gaps in their conceptual knowledge, the system becomes increasingly problematic. Often the identified whole school areas do not fully address the specific gaps in conceptual knowledge of each child, leading to further gaps developing.

In addition, unwittingly, the National Strategies' focus on layered curricular target setting seems to have opened the door for local authorities and publishing companies to promote set lists of layered curricular targets for different areas of the curriculum. The production and widespread marketing of such materials then restricts the ability of schools to engage meaningfully with the original concept. If, as busy practitioners, teachers can download a ready prepared set of layered curriculum targets, this will lead to the loss of any of the key benefits of developing whole school layered curricular target systems – including the need to rigorously analyse school-specific trends and patterns in underachievement and the opportunity to engage in reflective and productive professional dialogue.

Whole school layered curricular targets can be meaningful and effective within a school. However, this is dependent upon the individual school context and how staff use them. Simply implementing the whole school layered curricular targets as a system does not guarantee that there will be an impact upon pupil outcomes.

How can meaningful personalized targets be developed?

An effective and meaningful system must be developed for ensuring that class-based targets fully respond to individual pupils' specific learning needs. However, a balance needs to be met between responding fully to the personalization agenda and ensuring that the system that is developed does not become over-burdensome and time-consuming.

Where systems become over-burdensome and time-consuming, they often lead to reduced commitment to the system – too much time is put into setting the system up (to developing the personalized targets) and not enough is then put into ensuring that the targets are fully and appropriately supported and linked to whole-class teaching and learning opportunities on a day-to-day basis.

When a balance is achieved, this can lead to the evolution of highly appropriate and meaningful class-based targets to meet the needs of all children. The reading, writing, maths and science targets appropriately mirror the child's particular gaps and needs in specific areas of the curriculum – ensuring that meaningful progress can be made and supported within whole-class teaching and learning activities. Often, where such a system has been developed, targets for children with learning needs who are placed upon the SEN register can fully and appropriately respond to the individual and specific needs of the particular child within the class context, without the need for additional and separate targets and systems.

In such cases, where a rigorous system for writing and reviewing class-based targets has been set up which fully involves the pupils and parents in relevant discussions and planning, separate IEPs do not need to be written. The child's learning targets are fully met through the meaningful and personalized targets set through the whole-class target-setting process.

At this point, we should emphasize that by 'personalized' targets we do not mean (and neither does the government in its *2020 Vision* statement about personalized learning) that every child within the class will have his or her own very individual target. This would be unmanageable, leading to a system that would fail to meet the individual needs of any pupil.

Rather, targets should be responsive to pupils' actual needs, not just built around the decided target focus for that term. This can be effectively achieved through the production of group targets: often there are children working at similar levels and with similar needs in a particular curriculum area – and these children could then all be given the same, or a similar target. For this to work well, and to respond to the personalization agenda current today, it becomes essential for staff to ensure that children's strengths as well as weaknesses in curriculum areas are fully understood and acknowledged. Thus, a child may have a challenging group target in numeracy, to reflect his or her ability in this subject area, and a lower level group writing target to reflect his or her difficulties in that area.

Child-centred target setting – target setting for all pupils

How can all pupils be supported to engage in the target-setting process in a meaningful way?

We firmly believe that target setting is very important for focusing the attention of all involved in the education process upon the actual learning needs of every pupil at that time. The system that we described above for developing effective class-based targets relates not just to pupils with SEN, but also it clearly relates to how to think about ensuring that targets are meaningful and valuable for all pupils.

The key principle in all of this is that target setting must be a meaningful process. Staff need to be clear about why it is being done and how it supports their planning and teaching for the needs of all pupils. National Strategy guidance in recent years has emphasized that pupils need to know their targets (DCSF 2008) and so practice has generally evolved to develop systems such as sending out copies of a pupil's targets to parents, the production of target bookmarks, and target displays within classrooms.

Whilst this has been a welcome move and one which certainly helps to encourage shared ownership and knowledge of pupil targets, this alone is not enough to ensure that pupils are fully involved in target-setting systems. Indeed, in some schools we have been working with, pupils have noted that the target displays are so overly familiar that they are now not used effectively and that in fact they have lost their value or meaning. This is not the case in all schools. In some schools target displays are central and used effectively, but the key issue for staff is to understand that the display in itself will not foster commitment to the target. Where schools use targets and target displays to create a learning dialogue with pupils, then we have found there is more likely to be increases in pupil motivation and a sense of ownership of the learning process. This discussion can focus the attention of both pupil and teacher upon a particular aspect of the curriculum in which the pupil will work to improve during the target period.

Another simple factor which will improve the ability of all pupils to engage meaningfully with target setting is to ensure that the targets themselves are written in child-friendly, accessible language. This seems quite a common-sense principle – but it's potential impact is huge. Where schools have moved away from using jargon, where the tone of the targets is more personal: 'I will …' rather than 'to be able to …', pupils have noted a more positive and personal engagement with their targets. Pupils need to be able to understand, express and discuss their targets meaningfully with a range of people and it is therefore essential that they are given them in a format that they can understand and talk about.

Indeed, it is very important for pupils to be fully involved in meaningful discussions about the targets that are set and to have a voice in the choosing of the target. This not only allows pupils to gain some ownership of and commitment towards their learning but also gives the teacher an invaluable insight into the perspective of the pupil. Where we have seen this working well, this type of activity has been prioritized within the school setting, with time given to demonstrate the value that it holds for staff within the school setting.

Case study

Staff within the school noticed that after an initial increase in pupil engagement in their learning targets, pupils were starting to be less motivated by them. They became increasingly unable to talk meaningfully about their individual learning targets and this started to impact upon pupil progress in curriculum areas.

The leadership team raised this issue and decided to prioritize it as an area for whole school development within the next School Development Plan. Time was allocated during a staff INSET day at the beginning of the academic year for staff to thoroughly brainstorm current practice in target setting, and to reflect upon and suggest new ways forward.

Staff agreed a two-step approach to moving forward with target setting.

First, it was to become a whole-staff development target. All staff would have performance management targets set around the issue of meaningful target setting and staff meeting time would be allocated for staff discussion and further training about developing current target-setting practices. Staff also set up a working wall within the staff room on which every member of staff was asked to record both an example of when something to do with target setting had worked well and a new and innovative idea for how to develop target setting further.

Regular staff meeting time was set aside for a brief review and discussion about new items posted on the working wall. This had been the first time that this school had utilized a working wall within the staffroom (although it had been common practice within individual classrooms). Staff were excited by the idea, and used it well to record ideas and stimulate further thinking and innovation with each other. It helped to promote shared ownership of the principles around meaningful target setting.

Second, pupils were to become involved. All pupils were informed about the focus of discussions throughout the school during a whole school assembly and this was followed up by pupil discussions at regular intervals through the term.

These discussions gave pupils the opportunity to feed back to the teachers and staff about practices which helped them in relation to target setting. Staff were interested to note how much it was emphasized by pupils throughout the school that they wanted to be given the opportunity to explain to their teacher which aspects of learning they would like to focus upon – as pupils considered that this was often different to the aspect chosen by the class teacher.

Pupils also suggested the need to have regular brief progress review meetings with staff – so that both the staff member and the pupil could remember their target and become remotivated to make progress and achieve their target.

Target setting became the focus of an interactive pupil display within one of the corridors, where pupils were encouraged to post ideas about how to improve the current target-setting systems.

Over the year of the target-setting focus there was much change and development, culminating in the development of a clear system for giving pupils time to work individually with their class teacher to review their previous term's work and agree a target area to focus upon. Once targets were agreed and written up, the school focused upon giving ownership of the target to the pupil. Parents' afternoons were set up, where the focus of the afternoon was upon pupils having time to talk to their parents about the targets that had been set for them and how they were going to achieve them over the term.

Pupils, staff and parents were excited and motivated by the new target-setting systems – the targets were meaningful and pupils had direct ownership, ensuring increased commitment and motivation to achieve them.

Assessment for learning

What is assessment for learning?

Within this section of the chapter the key principles in relation to Assessment for Learning (QCA 2009) are going to be linked with the development of increasingly inclusive and meaningful target-setting systems to support all pupils. The Qualifications and Curriculum Authority in England define assessment for learning as follows:

> Assessment for learning involves using assessment in the classroom to raise pupils' achievement. It is based on the idea that pupils will improve most if they understand the aim of their learning, where they are in relation to this aim and how they can achieve the aim (or close the gap in their knowledge).

> (QCA 2009)

Our emphasis for assessment for learning within the context of meaningful target setting is upon supporting practitioners to utilize some of the principles to ensure that existing target-setting systems are enhanced within their school context.

It is not enough simply to set targets – for targets to be effective and meaningful they must be able to impact upon pupil progress and outcomes, and for this to happen there needs to be a continual cycle of assessment for (and of) learning.

It can become all too easy simply to focus upon the end outcome when setting targets. This, however, can lead to narrowed understanding of what is expected of the pupil, by the pupil, teacher and parent. Instead, we would encourage practitioners not only to consider the end point but to carefully plan the small steps of progress that will enable the pupil to make progress and achieve the given target.

How can teachers and pupils utilize aspects from an assessment for learning approach to enhance understanding of and commitment towards target setting?

Prior assessment of learning is essential to ensure that appropriate aspects of learning are targeted and that the targets and teaching do not simply reflect areas in which the child is already competent. This does not have to be time-consuming but should be built into teaching time before the introduction of a new teaching topic. Meaningful discussion of the prior assessment task with the pupil will help with the development of meaningful and appropriate agreed targets, with shared ownership and commitment between both teacher and pupil.

It is, then, essential not only to identify the area in need of improvement but also to explain clearly to the pupil what the end outcome is, what it may look like in practical terms and how the pupil can achieve this by working through a number of small steps. This process can help the target to seem more achievable to the pupil, as sometimes long-term targets with no indication of the small steps of progress that will build up to the target along the way can seem insurmountable.

It is essential to plan for regular times for staff members and pupils to come together to review the small steps progress, to note times when the pupil has skipped steps because of accelerated progress, to note how close to the end outcome the pupil has become and to review and compare work completed during the prior assessment task and now. This will support pupils in working effectively towards their end outcome targets.

This process should be developed into a meaningful and positive learning conversation with the pupil, in which the pupil is given the opportunity to voice the progress that he or she has made, to explain how certain steps have been achieved and to brainstorm collaboratively how to achieve next steps. Indeed, the very opportunity to vocalize thinking about the target helps both the pupil and the teacher towards greater and deeper understanding of the individual learning process of the particular pupil.

Concluding comments

Target setting is another key process within the interactive Inclusion in Action model that we present through this book. We see the target-setting process as a central part of the model which enables concrete action to take place. Target setting builds upon the other aspects of the model to enable the reflection, thinking and planning of data analysis, intervention planning and provision mapping to be translated into concrete targets for planning and practice.

Target setting is often a familiar process within the school context, but we would encourage staff to take time to critically question and reflect upon existing practices to consider whether they are still meaningful. Involving pupils and parents as a key part of this self-evaluation activity can add further insight into the process.

Where target-setting systems are set up that are fully inclusive, which respond to the learning needs of every child and which complement other systems, then the meaningful targets that are produced enable pupils to understand the learning process more fully, and teachers to respond more appropriately to the individual learning needs of all pupils.

Practitioners can use the following reflective questions as starting points for reviewing their own practice.

Reflective questions	Reflection/comment
What has this chapter taught me about inclusive target setting?	

How does this relate to my own current practice?	
How does this relate to current strategic practice in my school?	
What are the next steps in developing more inclusive target setting in my school?	

7   Final thoughts

In this chapter we critically explore the following issues and concepts:

- Understanding inclusive values
- Understanding and using the key principles and values within the Inclusion in Action model

At the heart of our model of Inclusion in Action are inclusive values and philosophies about how we can provide a meaningful school and learning experience for all pupils. The model builds upon these central principles by trying to embed the inclusive values into a range of essential but often taken-for-granted processes which occur within the school setting.

Having presented a clear discussion of the issues relating to these processes and how they can be viewed and enhanced through the Inclusion in Action model and approach to school development within the preceding chapters, in this final chapter, we wish to return to considering the inclusive values and to re-emphasize the key principles which are so central in underpinning our model.

Understanding inclusive values

A school should be a place which children enjoy being in, where they can learn together and explore the world around them. Schools should reflect the diversity of our communities and be part of the process of making those communities safe and equitable places to grow and develop as human beings. Schools should be places where children grow into adults, equipped with the values, skills, knowledge and understanding that will enable them to be full and active, caring and sensitive members of society.

Is this a vision of what schools might be like? Or what they should be like? In our work with schools we often ask teachers a series of questions:

1   What do you believe is the purpose of education – and what is your role in relation to that purpose?
2   What takes you out of bed every morning and into school to start your teaching?
3   What made you choose teaching as a profession?
4   Does your school ethos reflect your own personal values and beliefs about education and your role within it?

Responses may vary in small details but the answers are remarkably similar in their general content – teachers teach mostly because they love working with children, because they care about learning and because they want to make a contribution to the development of society. They want their schools to be places that children really enjoy coming to and where they learn as well and as much as they are able to. Interestingly, when we ask parents what they want from school for their children we get a very similar answer. Children, too, respond in the same way to this question.

So – schools should be places where children enjoy their learning and learn as well as they can. This sounds very familiar: the third outcome from Every Child Matters is that all children should 'enjoy and achieve' at school. Perhaps this is the simplest and best definition of an inclusive school – one which is striving to enable this to happen. Teachers, parents, children and even the government all seem to want the same thing.

How do we make this happen? 'Inclusive thinking and practice are hard work' said Len Barton (Armstrong and Moore 2004: 160). Creating and developing schools which achieve these very simple aims is a complex task and, as we have argued in this book, there is no set plan to follow. Inclusion is about many small and often apparently insignificant elements coming together to create places where everyone can learn together.

Interestingly it is when teachers respond to question 4, above, where they reflect on the ethos of the school in which they work, that their responses start to reflect the complexity of achieving enjoyment and achievement for all pupils in school. We have argued in this book that there is often a gulf between the details of inclusion policy and the realities of inclusive practice in and around classrooms.

Booth and Ainscow (2002: 7) argue that in order to develop inclusive schools, school development planning needs to pay attention to the three dimensions of:

- policy;
- practice;
- culture.

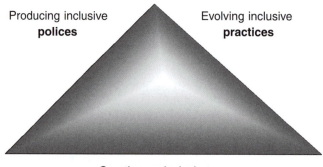

Producing inclusive **polices**

Evolving inclusive **practices**

Creating an inclusive **culture**

All three need to be developed together. If they are not, then schools will find that their rhetoric, in the form of policy, does not match their practice. The diagram above shows the model of the three dimensions from the Index for Inclusion (Booth and Ainscow 2002). Booth and Ainscow placed creating inclusive cultures along the base of the triangle because they believed that 'too little attention has been given to the potential for school cultures to support or undermine developments in teaching and learning' (Booth and Ainscow 2002: 7). We would go further and argue that if schools do not seek actively to create an inclusive culture, then there is no point trying to develop inclusive policies and there will be little evidence of inclusive practice in schools.

In this book we have introduced some approaches and ideas which we hope will support schools in creating an inclusive culture. Starting with a review of visions and values and the language that is used to describe the school's ethos will enable practitioners to begin thinking about the whole school and what it is seeking to achieve. Extend this discussion to the whole school community and there begins to be a developed understanding of a complex social setting where many diverse views and perspectives need to be somehow drawn together into a whole. And yet, as we argue above, mostly everyone wants the same things – it is in the discussion of the details that we need to start to explore and investigate collaborative ways forward.

Understanding and using the key principles and values within the Inclusion in Action model

Inclusion can only be developed through a whole school approach which draws together different systems and people into a coherent strategic process. The model of Inclusion in Action that we have discussed and developed within this book is one which, when prioritized within the school context, can lead to effective school development and change. In order for schools to be able to engage with the model in a meaningful way, they need to develop their understanding of the inclusive values which are so important to the model.

In particular, practitioners should be clear that the model:

- is built upon shared understanding of inclusive values and a commitment to continually evolving an inclusive culture within the school setting;
- acknowledges that every school is different and that any model of inclusive school development should therefore be developed and adapted to suit the particular needs of each school setting;
- is built upon an understanding that inclusion and inclusive practice is an ongoing process or journey – not an end state;
- emphasizes the importance of whole-staff ownership in and understanding of all of the school-based processes;

- emphasizes the importance of systems and processes being linked in dynamic and meaningful ways to enhance the overall effectiveness and impact on the educational experience and participation of every child.

To end, it is therefore useful for practitioners to review the principles that were set out in Chapter 1 when starting to explore what Inclusion in Action can look like within a school.

We would encourage practitioners to return to these principles now and to consider the extent to which they are currently a key part of their own school context, and possible ways to enhance or develop them further.

Inclusive principle: in my school, is/are there:	What evidence is there for this being prioritized and in place within my school setting? How could it be enhanced and developed further?
An inclusive culture which builds upon shared understanding of and commitment to inclusive values and practices?	
An ethos which is built upon removing barriers to participation, access and achievement for all pupils?	
School leaders who have a strong commitment to inclusive values – and is there evidence of distributed leadership across the school?	
An environment where all children can enjoy school and is the importance of this valued by everyone?	

A curriculum which has been designed to meet the needs of all?	
An environment where diversity is recognized and celebrated by all?	
Staff who are fully involved and work collaboratively together on whole school systems and processes which are linked in dynamic ways	
Ongoing professional and reflective dialogue which focuses on problem solving and developing creative approaches to curriculum innovation?	
Meaningful partnership working with parents and the local community which is prioritized by the school?	
A creative and professional approach to working collaboratively with a wide range of other professionals and agencies to support the needs of all pupils?	

Finally to all schools who are actively trying to develop more inclusive school cultures, policies and practices, we wish you all good luck and hope that this book has been of practical help to you.

Appendix 1

Hidden voices
The student voice activity

www.eenet.org.uk/key_issues/action/hidden_voices.shtml

Maggie Balshaw and Mel Ainscow

(The authors have given their permission to include this material.)

Introduction

The 'Hidden Voices' exercise was developed in Portugal by UNESCO consultants. It is an action research, or action learning, exercise. The action researchers can be external consultants, internal enquirers, or project coordinators. The words 'research' and 'action learning' have been omitted from these instructions in order to make them as user-friendly as possible. 'Information' has been used instead of 'data'.

A considerable amount of work had been done with the 'staff group', or teachers, before embarking upon this information-gathering exercise. The staff group had worked for two years on the development/implementation of their indicators of effective practice in developing more inclusive school contexts. Each indicator has a set of review questions to enable the gathering of information.

Aims:

- To gather the **views of students** about the developments the school has been involved in – specifically in relation to the school's **chosen indicators and review questions**.
- To use this evidence to compare with the evidence of the staff – using the evidence, or information, of the students.

You need to:

Choose groups of children to represent various year groups or classes in the school. These can be of mixed ages or same ages. Random choice is best.

You need small pieces of paper with 'Positive (+ve)' and 'Negative (–ve)' at the top for each group member, and a large piece of card with the statements written at the top (see diagram below). These statements are directly related to the school's.

Introduction to group of children

- We are here to think about how to improve the way the school feels to you.
- We/I want to listen to children's opinions and views.
- This is a private discussion. It will remain anonymous (explain).

- We will tell teachers about what has been said or written in the group, as they need to know what you think.

Stage 1: Children – writing

On these two pieces of paper are written two headings, for example:

- things that make you feel you want to go to lessons (+ve);
- things that make you feel you don't want to go to lessons (–ve).

Write down on each piece of paper what you want to say. One thing on each piece of paper is fine, more if you want. Don't talk. No discussion to begin with. Write for yourself.

When they seem ready, check if they need help.

Let's start by reading the first one. Each student reads so all can hear.

When each has had their turn:

Put them down here together so all can be seen.

Things that make you feel you want to …	Things that make you feel you don't want to …
+ve	–ve

Let's have a conversation …

- Do we agree with all the others?
- Take a turn each to say what you think about what others have written. Do you agree?
- Does anyone really disagree and what makes you think that?

Do exactly the same with the negative (–ve) ones; make notes as the children make significant comments.

Stage 2: Children – further questions

Probe more deeply using the school's chosen indicators and questions that you feel the children may be able to respond to. (Of course, some questions may not be relevant to them.)

These are some examples chosen in a school where the following issues were key:

- What are the rules you have to follow?
- What happens if children experience difficulties in lessons?
- What do teachers do to encourage children to come to lessons?

Make notes of the children's responses to the indicator issues. Finish off by thanking them. Say how important it is that we listen to what they have to say. The teachers will hear what the group thinks and says, but not what individuals said.

Stage 3: Staff analysis and discussion

The information for the staff to discuss and analyse is as follows:

- the children's notes;
- the comments recorded from the conversations which took place in Stage 2.

Before the discussion:

- keep the children's positive and negative papers together.
- take the additional notes recorded during the discussion with the children and cut them into individual strips.

1 To engage the staff group with the children's writing

- Give each small staff group a selection of the children's own writing to consider. (No more than 3–4 people in each group.)
- Ask them about what they take as significant messages from these issues – positive and negative.
- Ask them to record key points.

2 To engage the staff group in a more detailed analysis of the information provided by the children

- Give them the notes about the children's comments on the positive (+ve) and negative (–ve) papers, and on the school's indicators and review questions. (The comments should be cut up into strips and randomly distributed.)
- Ask them to write two headings:
  - the school's indicators;
  - the review questions.

- Then allocate the children's views, as appropriate.

Questions to think about

These questions can be used with coordination teams:

- What do the children say?
- Are there any patterns?
- Are there any contradictions?
- What does this information make us consider?
- Can we use it to strengthen our strategy?
- How can we use the children's information to involve our colleagues in the school?

These can be used in a whole school staff meeting:

- What is significant about the information collected?

- What messages should the adults in the school be taking from what the children had to say?
- What are the similarities and differences (correlation/dissonance) with the adults' views?
- What should be done by:
  - teachers and teaching assistants;
  - managers;
  - children/students;
  - others?

With the whole group

Draw out the key findings from each indicator, or from the review questions, into the whole group. Make a record on a flipchart and then identify action points. Or, you can listen to the feedback and make a record of it (collate) after the meeting. Written feedback should be disseminated after the meeting. And another meeting should be arranged to deal with the findings and to do some further review and action planning.

Appendix 2.1

Example format to enable careful planning of specific interventions

Class Focus of Intervention	
The pupils	
Who is the intervention aimed at?	
Why is it aimed at these pupils?	(e.g. evidence from assessment results*/ impact on learning …)
What do you expect the pupils to achieve as a result of the intervention?	(e.g. a clear rationale/reason for choosing this intervention)
Assessing skill levels	
What will be the entry criteria for this intervention?	
How will baseline skill level be assessed and measured?	
What will be the exit criteria for the intervention?	
How will exit skill level be measured?	

Delivery	
How long will the intervention run for?	
Who will deliver the intervention?	
When?	
Where?	
Monitoring progress	
How will the teacher monitor progress on a weekly basis?	
How will be progress be monitored?	
Who will monitor daily progress?	
How will progress be measured/recorded when it is transferred into the whole context?	
How will the children be able to monitor and evaluate their own progress?	
Are any resources needed? Do they need to be found/ made?	

Is any further support needed e.g. from outside agency professionals?	

Appendix 2.2

Example format for reviewing progress halfway through intervention programmes: ensuring progress

The group and individual targets and interventions are now nearly halfway through their specified time allocation. We need to start thinking now about the progress that pupils are making so that we can identify anything that is currently stopping the pupils from making progress. We can also think about what we need to do now to ensure that they do achieve the outcomes that we set for them by the end of the intervention period.

Are there any targets where the pupil(s) is (are) not achieving orange or green (achieving or nearly achieving the target)? Please list.	
What is stopping them from achieving a green? For example, is it concentration/ behaviour/non-attendance/skill is too complex for them …	
Is there anything that we could do *now* to help the pupil(s) to get a green?	

Appendix 2.3

Example weekly group intervention monitoring form

This uses a traffic light system to record progress: red = no progress towards measureable outcome; orange = making progress towards measureable outcome; green = measureable outcome achieved.

Week beginning: 28.1.09 end of week evaluation	Child A	Child B	Child C	Child D	Child E	Child F
To be able to structure a sentence correctly, so that it makes sense and is punctuated correctly						
To be able to put simple adjectives into a sentence to add interest						
To use and spell National Curriculum high frequency words confidently						
To know how to start sentences in different ways						
To use ! and ? correctly at the ends of sentences						
To punctuate direct speech correctly						
To use but, so, when, then and because to connect sentences						

Week beginning: 23.3.09 end of week evaluation	Child A	Child B	Child C	Child D	Child E	Child F
To be able to structure a sentence correctly, so that it makes sense and is punctuated correctly	Absent					
To be able to put simple adjectives into a sentence to add interest	Absent					
To use and spell National Curriculum high frequency words confidently	Absent					
To know how to start sentences in different ways	Absent					
To use ! and ? correctly at the ends of sentences	Absent					
To punctuate direct speech correctly	Absent					
To use but, so, when, then and because to connect sentences	Absent					

Appendix 2.4

Example end of intervention review format

Pupil: Child A

Period of intervention   **From: September 2008**

To: December 2008

Review of targets (Red: target not achieved; Yellow: target nearly achieved; Green: target achieved)

1 I will spell 80 high frequency words correctly.
2 I will spell words using sh, ch and th sounds.
3 I will be able to use word endings -ed and -ing correctly in my writing.
4 I will independently structure three sentences using full stops, finger spaces and one interesting adjective.
5 I will make sure that all my letters are correctly formed and positioned on the line and that I use capital letters correctly.

General comments

Strengths and progress made during the intervention / what works well:

Any continuing areas of difficulty:

Possible next steps:

List of abbreviations used in example provision maps

ALS   Additional Literacy Strategy
CLO   Children's Liaison Officer
CT   Class teacher
EAL   Pupils with English as an additional language
HA   Higher ability
LA   Lower ability
MA   Middle ability
NC   National Curriculum
RHF   Reception high-frequency words
SEBD   Social, emotional and behavioural difficulties
S&L   Speech and language
TA   Teaching assistant

Appendix 3.1

Example primary provision map format:

Year 4	Provision/resource	Staff/pupil ratio	Staff involved	Cost in time (termly)	Type of group
Reading	1:1 reading every other day.	1:1	CT/TA	Every other day	All
	Focused reinforcement of Reception high-frequency words	1:3	CT/TA	Daily	Lower ability
	Use of reading recovery strategies	1:1	CT/TA	Daily	Lower ability
	Phonic games/intervention programme	1:5	CT/TA	Daily	Lower ability
	Differentiated reading comprehension	1:4	CT/TA	3 x weekly	Middle ability/ Higher ability
	Phonic/intervention programme	1:5	CT/TA	Daily	Lower ability
	Vocabulary reinforcement/practice	1:2	CT/TA	Daily	English as an additional language
Writing	Phonics programme	1:4	CT/TA	Daily	Lower ability
	Spelling practice	1:6	CT/TA	Daily	All
	Handwriting practice	All	CT/TA	Daily	All
	ALS	1:6	CT/TA	3 x weekly	Middle ability
Numeracy	Wave 3 numeracy	1:4	CT/TA	3 x weekly	Lower ability
	Times-tables practice	1:6	CT/TA	Daily	All

Appendix 3.2

Example secondary provision map format

Year 10

Provision/ resource	Staff/student ratio	Staff involved	Cost in time (termly)	Outcomes
Anger management groups	6:1	Social, emotional and behavioural difficulties support teacher	16 x 50 mins	
Alternative curriculum group 1	10:1	Support teacher	15 x 50 mins	
Connexions – mentoring	1:1	Careers adviser	6 x 50 mins	
Part-time college placements (15 pupils)	3:15	Teaching assistant/teacher	6 x 50 mins	
In-class support		Teaching assistant	26 x 50 mins	
Touch typing training	1:1	Teaching assistant	15 x 20 mins	
Homework support	10:1	Pastoral support teacher	Daily	
Speech and language therapy	1:1	Speech and language therapist	6 x 30 mins	

Appendix 3.3

Example Wave 1 provision map linked to pupil progress review meetings

Class: **Date:**

Area of need/gap	Current level	Expected level	Pupils requiring specific intervention	Identified provision/resource to meet need	Staff/pupil ratio	Cost in time / staff involved
Behaviour/ planning for the day			All	Visual timetable	2:28	Daily CT & TA
Punctuation	2c–4c	3b–3a	All	Focus on punctuation in all lessons Daily punctuation game	2:28	Daily CT & TA
Writing	2c–4c	3b–3a	Lower ability and middle ability (LA and MA) Higher ability (HA): extension work in a small group	Timetabled times for main lesson to be pitched to respond to needs of LA HA to access extension group activity	2:22 1:6	2 x weekly CT, TA and Learning Mentor
Writing	2c–4c	3b–3a	All	Focus on description and content in writing Daily reviews of work to add to working wall display	2:28	Daily CT & TA

Reading	2c–4c	3b–3a	LA and MA	Reading comprehension activities at an appropriate level HA – extended reading activity	2:20 1:10	3 x weekly CT, TA and Learning Mentor
Independent learning skills	2c–4c	3b–3a	All	2 afternoons of problem-solving project work to encourage thinking skills and independent learning skills based around maths, literacy and ICT	2:28	2pms x weekly
Social skills and work motivation	2c–4c	3b–3a	All	Social skills support during learning activities Children's Liaison Officer working with one group	1:6	Daily children's Liaison Officer

Appendix 3.4

Example Wave 2 provision map linked to pupil progress review meetings

Class: **Date:**

Area of need/gap	Current level	Expected Level	Pupils requiring specific intervention	Identified provision/resource to meet need	Staff/pupil ratio	Cost in time / staff involved
Ability to use different genres of writing in own writing	3c–3b	3b–3a		Small-group reinforcement of different writing styles and genres	1:6	3 × weekly CT/TA
Reading	2a–3c	3b–3a		Better Reading Partnerships	1:1	3 × weekly trained TA
Numeracy – boost to reach age appropriate	3c	3b–3a		Springboard	1:5	Daily CT/TA

Appendix 3.5

Example Wave 3 provision map linked to pupil progress review meetings

Class: **Date:**

Area of need/gap	Current level	Expected level	Pupils requiring specific intervention	Identified provision/resource to meet need	Staff/pupil ratio	Cost in time/staff involved
Reading	1b–2c	3b–3a		Wave 3 Better Reading Partnerships	1:1	Daily Reading Recovery teacher and trained TAs
Maths	2c	3b–3a		Wave 3 Maths with mental maths questions/focus	1:5	3 x weekly CT/TA
Writing	2b	3b–3a		Vocabulary and sentence structure work	1:3	Daily Learning Mentor/CT
Behaviour				Clear school expectations and link with mum. Home–school behaviour agreement	1:1	Daily CT/TA Speech and Language Therapist mum
Learning		3b–3a		Focus on encouraging independent working. Reward system	1:1	Daily x 10 min activity CT/TA
Writing	1a–2b	3b–3a		Basic sentence construction. Adult to check evey piece of independent work with child	1:4/1:1	Daily CT/TA

Appendix 4

Example daily target tracking format: ongoing progress tracking

Name of child:	
Start date: September 2008	**End date: December 2008**

Date	*Targets (Highlight in red/amber/green to show progress)*	*Comments/evidence*
	1 I will read 100 words by sight 2 I will write 1 sentence carefully by myself so that I can read it back to an adult without help 3 I will use prompt cards to help me to remember key instructions and routines 4 I will be able to get out and put away my equipment independently within 2 minutes 5 I will listen to and respond sensibly and politely to adults	
	1 I will read 100 words by sight 2 I will write 1 sentence carefully by myself so that I can read it back to an adult without help 3 I will use prompt cards to help me to remember key instructions and routines 4 I will be able to get out and put away my equipment independently within 2 minutes 5 I will listen to and respond sensibly and politely to adults	

References

Ainscow, M. (1999) *Understanding the Development of Inclusive Schools*. London: Routledge.

Ainscow, M., Booth, T., Dyson, A. *et al.* (2006) *Improving Schools, Developing Inclusion*. London: Routledge.

Armstrong, F. and Moore, M. (2004) *Action Research for Inclusive Education: Changing Places, Changing Practices, Changing Minds*. London: Routledge.

Arthur, C. and Kallick, B. (1993) Through the lens of a critical friend, *Educational Leadership*, 51(2): 49–51.

Balshaw, M. and Ainscow, M. (1998) *Hidden Voices*, www.eenet.org.uk/key_issues/action/hidden_voices.shtml (accessed 24 February 2009).

Barton, L. (1997). Inclusive education: romantic, subversive or realistic? *International Journal of Inclusive Education*, 1(3): 231–42.

Black-Hawkins, K., Florian, L., Rouse, M. *et al.* (2007) *Achievement and Inclusion in Schools*. London: Routledge.

Booth, T. and Ainscow, M. (2000, 2008) *Breaking Down the Barriers: The Index for Inclusion*. www.csie.org.uk/publications/breaking-barriers.shtml (accessed 22 February 2009).

Booth, T. and Ainscow, M. (2002) *Index For Inclusion*. Bristol: Centre for Studies in Inclusive Education.

Booth, T. and Black-Hawkins, K. (2001, 2005) *Developing Learning and Participation in Countries of the South: The Role of an Index for Inclusion*. Paris: UNESCO.

Carrington, S. and Robinson, S. (2006) Inclusive school community: why is it so complex? *International Journal of Inclusive Education*, 10(4–5): 323–34.

Chitty, C. (1996) Ruskin's legacy, *TES Magazine*, 18 October.

Corbett, J. (2001) *Supporting Inclusive Education: A Connective Pedagogy*. London: RoutledgeFalmer.

DCSF (Department for Children, Schools and Families) (2007a) *A New Relationship with Schools: The School Improvement Partner's Brief. Advice and Guidance on the role of the School Improvement Partner*. SIP Brief Edition 3. London: DCSF.

DCSF (Department for Children, Schools and Families) (2007b) *The Children's Plan*. London: DCSF.

DCSF (Department for Children, Schools and Families) (2007c) *P Scales Guidance, 2009*, www.nationalstrategies.standards.dcsf.gov.uk/node/116682 (accessed 16 February 2009).

DCSF (Department for Children, Schools and Families) (2007d) *Primary National Strategy: Pupil Progress Meetings Prompts and Guidance.* London: The Stationery Office.

DCSF (Department of Education and Skills) (2008) *The National Strategies,* www.nationalstrategies.standards.dcsf.gov.uk (accessed 16 February 2009).

DES (Department of Education and Science) (1993) *Special Educational Needs Code of Practice on the Identification and Assessment of Special Educational Needs.* London: DES.

DES (Department of Education and Science) (1999) *The National Curriculum Key Stage 1 and 2.* London: DES.

DfES (Department for Education and Skills) (2001) *Special Educational Needs Code of Practice.* London: DfES.

DfES (Department for Education and Skills) (2002) *Primary National Strategy in England.* London: DfES.

DfES (Department for Education and Skills) (2003) *Secondary National Strategy in England.* London: DfES.

DfES (Department for Education and Skills) (2004a) *Using Curricular Targets.* London: DfES.

DfES (Department for Education and Skills) (2004b) *Children Act.* London: The Stationery Office.

DfES (Department for Education and Skills) (2004c) *Removing Barriers to Achievement: The Government's Strategy for SEN.* London: The Stationery Office.

DfES (Deparment for Education and Skills) (2005) *Leading On Inclusion.* London: DfES.

DfES (Department for Education and Skills (2006a) *2020 Vision.* Report of the Teaching and Learning in 2020 Review Group. London: Crown Publications.

DfES (Department for Education and Skills) (2006b) *Strengthening Teaching and Learning Through the Use of Curricular Targets: Primary National Strategy.* London: DfES.

DfES (Department for Education and Skills (2006c) *Leading on Intervention.* London: DfES.

Doreman, T., Deppeler, J. and Harvey, D. (2005) *Inclusive Education: A Practical Guide to Supporting Diversity in the Classroom.* London: RoutledgeFalmer.

Durrant, J. and Holden, G. (2005) *Teachers Leading Change: Doing Research for School Improvement.* London: Paul Chapman Publishers.

Dyson, A., Howes, A. and Roberts, B. (2002) *A Systematic Review of the Effectiveness of School-level Actions for Promoting Participation by All Students* (EPPI Centre Review). Research Evidence in Education Library, Issue 1. London: EPPI Centre, Social Science Research Unit, Institute of Education.

Ellis, S., Tod, J. and Graham-Matheson, L. (2008) *Special Needs and Inclusion: Reflection and Renewal.* Birmingham: NASUWT.

Grimes, P. (2009) *A Quality Education For All: The History of the Lao PDR Inclusive Education Project 1993–2009.* Vientiane: Save the Children.

Gross, J. (2008) *Beating Bureaucracy in Special Educational Needs*. London: Routledge.

Gross, J. and White, A. (2003) *SEN and School Improvement*. London: David Fulton Publishers.

Hanko, G. (1995) *Special Needs in Ordinary Classrooms: From Staff Support to Staff Development*, 3rd edn. London: David Fulton Publishers.

Hanko, G. (1999) *Increasing Competence through Collaborative Problem Solving*. London: David Fulton Publishers.

Hart, S. (1996) *Beyond Special Needs: Enhancing Children's Learning through Innovative Thinking*. London: Sage Publications.

Hart, S., Dixon, A., Drummond, M. J. *et al.* (2004). *Learning Without Limits*. Maidenhead: Open University Press.

Hopkins, D. (2007) *Every School a Great School*. Maidenhead: Open University Press.

House of Commons, Education and Skills Committee (2006) *Special Educational Needs*, Third Report of Session 2005–06. London: The Stationery Office.

Jones, J. and Hennessy-Jones, M. (2003) Practitioner critical friendship: a major contribution to school capacity building. Paper presented to 16th International Congress for School Improvement and Effectiveness, Sydney, 5–8 January.

Kugelmass, J. (2004) *The Inclusive School: Sustaining Equity and Standards*. New York: Teachers College Press.

MacBeath, J. (1999) *Schools Must Speak for Themselves: The Case for Self-evaluation*. London: Routledge.

MacBeath, J. (2006) *School Inspection and Self-evaluation: Working with the New Relationship*. London: RoutledgeFalmer.

MacBeath, J., Galton, M., Steward, M. *et al.* (2005) *The Costs of Inclusion: A Study of Inclusion Policy and Practice in English Primary, Secondary and Special Schools*. London: National Union of Teachers.

MacBeath, J., Gray, J. M., Cullen, J. *et al.* (2007) *Schools on the Edge: Responding to Challenging Circumstances*. London: Paul Chapman.

Macbeath, J. and McGlynn, A. (2002) *Self-Evaluation: What's In It for Schools?* London: Routledge.

Morley, A. (2006) The development of leadership capacity in a school facing challenging circumstances, in M. Ainscow and M. West (eds), *Improving Urban Schools: Leadership and Collaboration*. Maidenhead: Open University Press.

NCSL (National College for School Leadership) (2004) *Distributed Leadership*. Nottingham: NCSL.

Ofsted (Office for Standards in Education) (2004a) *SEN and Disability: Towards Inclusive Schools*. London: Ofsted.

Ofsted (2004b) *A New Relationship with Schools*. London: Ofsted.

Ofsted (2005) *The Framework for Inspecting Schools in England from September 2005*. London: Ofsted.

Ofsted (2006a) *Inclusion: Does it Matter Where Pupils are Taught? An Ofsted Report on the Provision and Outcomes in Different Settings for Pupils with Learning Difficulties and Disabilities.* London: Ofsted.

Ofsted (2006b) *Best Practice in Self-evaluation.* London: Ofsted.

Peters, S. (2003) *Inclusive Education: Achieving Education for All by Including Those with Disabilities and Special Educational Needs.* Geneva: World Bank.

Pirrie, A., Head, G. and Brna, P. (2006) *Mainstreaming Pupils with Special Educational Needs: An Evaluation.* Edinburgh: Scottish Executive Education Department.

QCA (Qualifications and Curriculum Authority) (2009) *Assessment for Learning,* www.qca.org.uk/qca_4334.aspx (accessed 17 January 2009).

Rieser, R. and Mason, M. (1992) *Disability Equality in the Classroom: A Human Rights Issue.* London: Disability Equality in Education.

Sherman, R. R. and Webb, R. B. (1988) *Qualitative Research in Education: Focus and Methods.* London: RoutledgeFalmer.

Singal, N. (2005) Mapping the field of inclusive education: a review of the Indian literature, *International Journal of Inclusive Education,* 9(4): 331–50.

Singal, N. and Rouse, M. (2003) We do inclusion: practitioner perspectives in some inclusive schools in India, *Perspectives in Education,* 21(3).

Slee, R. (2004) Inclusive education: a framework for reform, in V. Heung and M. Ainscow (eds), *Inclusive Education: A Framework for Reform?* Hong Kong: Hong Kong Institute of Education.

Stoll, L. and Fink, D. (1989) *Changing Our Schools: Linking School Effectiveness and School Improvement.* Maidenhead: Open University Press.

Swaffield, S. (2002) Contextualising the work of the critical friend. Paper presented to 15th International Congress for School Effectiveness and Improvement (ICSEI), Copenhagen, 3–6 January.

Swaffield, S. (2004) Exploring critical friendship through leadership for learning. Paper presented at 17th International Congress for School Improvement and Effectiveness (ICSEI), Rotterdam, 6–9 January.

TDA (Teacher Development Agency) (2007) *School Improvement Planning Framework,* www.tda.gov.uk/remodelling/extendedschools/sipf2.aspx (accessed 7 May 2009).

UN (United Nations) (1989) *Convention on the Rights of the Child.* New York: United Nations.

UNESCO (1994) *The Salamanca Statement and Framework for Action on Special Needs Education.* Adopted by the World Conference on Special Needs Education: Access and Quality, Salamanca, 7–10 June.

UNESCO (2008) Education For All by 2015: will we make it? Summary. *EFA Global Monitoring Report.* Paris: UNESCO.

Warnock, M. (1978) *Warnock Report: Special Educational Needs.* Report of the Committee of Enquiry into the education of handicapped children and young people. London: HMSO.

Wrigley, T. (2003) *Schools of Hope: A New Agenda for School Improvement.* Stoke on Trent: Trentham Books.

Index

DECONSTRUCTING SPECIAL EDUCATION AND CONSTRUCTING INCLUSION 2/E

Gary Thomas and Andrew Loxley

Reviews of the first edition:

'... full of sparkling analysis ... an absorbing account of how and why the practice of special education has failed to live up to expectations.'
Dr Caroline Roaf, British Journal of Educational Studies

'... a sophisticated, multidisciplinary critique of special education that leaves virtually no intellectual stone unturned. '
Professor Tom Skrtic, University of Kansas, USA

'While this is a weighty book, there is real clarity about the key ideas and no doubting their importance.'
Dr Melanie Nind in Times Educational Supplement

"... a striking ... thought-provoking yet lyrical account which is both uncompromising in its stance and refreshing in its intellectually sophisticated critique."
Professor Phil Garner in British Journal of Special Education

Review of the second edition:

'Having read this book with much pleasure when it first came out in 2001, I am delighted to see its authors rewarded with the accolade of a second edition. Indeed it has been an equally agreeable experience to revisit it, and interesting too, since there have been some significant shifts in thinking in the intervening years.'
Support for Learning · Volume 23 · Number 2 · 2008

In the second edition of this best-selling text, the authors critically examine the intellectual foundations of special education and consider the consequences of their influence for professional and popular thinking about learning difficulties. In light of this critique, they suggest that much of the knowledge about special education is misconceived, and proceed to provide a powerful rationale for inclusion derived from ideas about social justice and human rights.

Revised and updated throughout, the book contains new material on social capital, communities of practice and a 'psychology of difference', as well as a new chapter on 'Inclusive education for the twenty-first century'.

Deconstructing Special Education and Constructing Inclusion is essential reading for teachers, head teachers, educational psychologists and policy makers.

Contents: Special education: Theory and theory talk – The knowledge-roots of special education – The great problem of 'need': A case study in children who don't behave – Thinking about learning failure, especially in reading – Modelling difference – Inclusive schools in an inclusive society? Policy, politics and paradox – Constructing inclusion – Inclusive education for the twenty-first century: Histories of help; hopes for respect.

2007   176pp

978-0-335-22371-8 (Paperback)   978-0-335-22370-1 (Hardback)

A BEGINNING TEACHER'S GUIDE TO SPECIAL EDUCATIONAL NEEDS

Janice Wearmouth

'This is a refreshing and comprehensive book providing an excellent introduction to theory and practice in SEN. It will be much in demand and appreciated by all teachers who are attempting to tackle the issues and questions that can accompany the desire to meet the learning needs of all children.'

> *Dr. Gavin Reid, Educational Consultant, Red Rose School, UK; Centre for Child Evaluation and Teaching, Kuwait; REACH Learning Center, Canada.*

As a trainee or newly qualified teacher, being faced with students labelled as having 'special educational needs' can be a daunting prospect. The whole area of SEN and 'inclusion' is often shrouded with uncertainty about what it means, either in theory or in practice, and what it entails.

This guide addresses these issues in a straightforward, supportive and practical way, focusing on the needs of the beginning teacher. Using case studies, activities and resources, it will equip you with the skills and knowledge to support groups of pupils with SEN in different settings and phases.

Key features include:

- Vignettes to illustrate the kinds of challenges you are likely to face in ensuring that all students can learn effectively in their classrooms
- Clarification of the legal responsibilities of all teachers in relation to special needs provision
- An overview of the four broad areas of need outlined in the Special Educational Needs Code of Practice (DfES, 2001), including strategies appropriate to each
- A discussion of assessment and planning, including student, peer and family views
- Focus on difficulties in the area of numeracy and literacy, including effective intervention strategies
- Coverage of behavioural issues and effective resolution strategies
- An insight into the uses of ICT to support students' learning and achievement
- Sources of further specialist advice and support

A Beginning Teacher's Guide to Special Educational Needs provides essential support and guidance for student teachers during and beyond their teaching training.

Contents: *Section I Special educational needs: Policy and context – Making sense of learning and difficulties in learning – A historical perspective and the current legal position – Section II Approaches to assessment, planning, teaching and learning – Overview of approaches to four areas of need – Assessment and planning – Addressing the needs of learners who experience literacy difficulties – Understanding and addressing special difficulties in mathematics – Behavioural issues in classrooms – Section III Support for special learning needs – Uses of ICT to support students' special learning needs – Professional relationships with other people.*

2008   256pp

978-0-335-23354-0 (Paperback)   978-0-335-23352-6 (Hardback)